PRISON TO THE PALACE

A JOURNEY TO FREEDOM

First Published in Great Britain in 2024

All emphasis within Scripture quotations is the author's own. Please note that the name satan and related names are not capitalised. This has been the author's choice however the author recognises that it is grammatically incorrect.

ISBN: 978-1-8380446-9-5

Published by Alan Searle Media in the United Kingdom for worldwide distribution, to glorify Christ through creative writing and truthful testimony. Online at http://alansearle.media

Cover design by Lawson Design

Acknowledgements

This book would not have been possible without the support and belief of my amazing wife, Laura, who has also been a great help with the editing. Thank you for your continued support.

Thank you also to all those who helped with proof reading. This book would not be the same without you.

I also want to thank all those who encouraged me to write a second book, for your continued belief in me.'

Finally, I dedicate this book to Father God, without You this book would never have been written. May this give You all the glory.

About the Author

Mark is passionate about people living from the revelation of God as their perfect loving Father and our identity as beloved children of God. Mark longs to see people receive inner healing and walk in the freedom of personal wholeness.

After graduating from Bible College, Mark has been involved in Christian ministry over the last 20 years including a number of years serving in Malawi. Mark and his wife are based in Devon and serve together in their home church, where amongst other things they offer Bethel Sozo (inner healing) and Father Heart Days.

Mark is the author of 'In His Image: Rediscovering Who We Are.'

If you would like more information about Mark's ministry or want to get in touch, please head to his website at www.markandlaura.co.uk.

Contents

Endorsements

In writing "Prison to the Palace" Mark has written another very practical book on how we can have a deeper relationship with the Father, Son and Holy Spirit. Life throws a lot of negative things at us, often whilst we are in our childhood. These stick to us and shape who we are: our perceptions, beliefs and even our view of God. They form the prison that prevents us living in the glorious freedom that belongs to sons and daughters of the Father.

Mark carefully highlights many of the things that have put us, and keep us, in prison.

And there is hope! We do not have to stay that way.

Without condemnation or judgement, Mark highlights various keys that we can take hold of in order to open the prison doors and escape from the grasp of the enemy. Sometimes it may not be easy and we may need help but persevering will lead us into freedom.

By taking these practical steps we can begin to find our true home in the Father's presence. We find the Palace.

For anyone struggling with their identity, feeling distant from God or just aware that there must be more of God to experience, this book is a must read.

Mark Gyde
A Father to YOU
https://afathertoyou.com

Mark Russell's latest book… Prison to the Palace, is a very helpful resource for all who desire to go deeper into their relationship with God but may sometimes feel stuck.

Mark does a fantastic job of describing the things common to all of us that can often cause us to feel unable to enter into the fullness of life that Jesus secured for us. He also provides very practical keys that will help each reader find the freedom they are searching for in Christ.

So, if you long to experience the immeasurable ocean of the Father's amazing love in increasing measure and be freed from some of the things that might hinder you in your journey, I highly recommend this book.

Barry Adams
Author: 'Father's Love Letter'

Introduction

Have you ever reflected on your life and identified a pattern of going round and round with the same issue or the same thought patterns - negative thoughts about who you are? These thought patterns seem to influence who you are, they appear to hold you back and, as a result, you have some negative feelings about your life. Do you have thoughts that seem to dominate and that stop you moving forward? These thoughts keep you from your destiny.

Perhaps you often look at others and it seems like no one else feels this way. It appears that everyone else has their lives all together; they don't suffer the way you do. I want to encourage you – you are not alone. Unfortunately, however, with these feelings we begin to have thoughts that further solidifies our beliefs about who we think we are. We think that others couldn't possibly understand us or sympathise with what we are feeling and going through. In turn, you begin to feel more alone, more unloved, more pessimistic. As this happens, you can then find yourself withdrawing from family, friends, and others. You become even more inward looking.

I hope, that through reading this book, you will begin to believe and understand that these thoughts are lies and that there is a way out. My prayer is that, as you read these pages, you will discover vital keys to unlock you from the prison and open up the place where God intends you to live from: the palace.

Paul teaches in his letter to the Ephesians:

'And God ***raised*** *us up with Christ and* ***seated*** *us with Him in the Heavenly realms in Christ Jesus.'*

Ephesians 2:6 (emphasis added)

Throughout this verse, Paul is talking in the past tense – we have *already* been seated with Christ. It is not just something we can look forward to; it has already happened! If we are already seated in Heavenly places, then we should be able to live in that place now. Surely it is possible to live in the palace whilst we are alive on the earth. I am not suggesting we don't live trouble-free lives or that we never face hardships. What I am suggesting, however, is that we can expect to live from a different perspective: we can live from the perspective of Heaven. Some of us may not always be living from the perspective of Heaven. We are not living in the palace; we are all too often still living from a prison. Therefore, if we are living from a place of false understanding and believing the lies of the enemy, then we are not fully living as Father intended us to. We are not fully embracing our destiny. If it's truly possible to no longer live in this prison and to live instead from the palace of truth – a place of security – then how can we do that? How do we move from living in the prison to living as we were designed to live; living as though we really are seated with Him in the palace?

This book contains keys that will unlock you from the prison and help move you into the palace. For too long, many of us have lived in the prison without realising that we already have the keys to be able to free ourselves. God is so good that He doesn't expect us to read verses like the one quoted above and then for us to struggle to free ourselves to no avail. When God declares something, such as this verse, He also gives us everything we need to live in that reality. Knowing and understanding the keys enables us to really live as He intended us to live. The perspective on earth is not the reality of living in Heaven.

Father began to speak to me about writing this book after my first book: 'In His Image: Rediscovering Who We Are' was published. Within a week of publication, I began to have thoughts of not feeling good enough and of having nothing valid to say. As a result, I began to ask myself "*will anyone even want to read my book*?" I started to question His call on my life and, pessimistically, questioned what I knew God had called me to do. I reverted to my old way of thinking from before I began my journey into encountering Father's heart towards me.[1] It didn't matter when people said something positive – I was able to turn positives around in my head and hear a negative side. I

[1]For more on this read my book 'In His Image: Rediscovering Who We Are.'

felt, once again, locked into that way of thinking. Had I really made any progress in my mindset? Was my mind really being renewed? I even questioned the journey I had written about, struggling to believe it in my heart or indeed experience it. A friend spotted my thought patterns and asked me "*When did you begin to think like this? Haven't you just published a book on this very subject?*" I suddenly realised that what I was feeling was a direct attack from the enemy – and I had started to believe the lies that I thought I had overcome and moved on from. Despite this, I was unsure how to move out of this situation. I tried… I prayed… but the more I did, the deeper I was sliding back into my old way of thinking. I was thinking like an orphan again and operating out of an orphan mindset. I was once again needing approval from others. Even when I received that approval, I wasn't able to accept it. Despite encouraging feedback and testimonies, I dismissed them as people just being kind or not really meaning what they were saying. I was unable to see or hear what others thought and said about me or the book. It felt like I had lost who I thought I was. The enemy was attacking the very thing that I thought I felt secure in: I had lost the identity that I had written about.

As I listened to Father, He began to show me that I had the keys to be able to move back into the palace. He explained that once we have moved from the prison to the palace then we are able – even though we feel we are still struggling – to live back in the palace. He revealed to me that although our minds may be feeling bound up again, our hearts are free, and it is possible to get to that place of living in the palace.

This book is in three distinct parts:

Prison

If we're on a journey, then the prison could be understood to be the current location – it is the starting point. We all start from different locations. What specific things have imprisoned you? What are the effects of this on you and your thinking? I'll be showing you how to unpack 'prison thinking', unpick how these thoughts are holding you back, and then invite you to change the prison mindset. For example, prison thinking of being trapped by hopelessness and imprisoned by its effect can be changed to what palace thinking would look like – living a life of hope. It stands to reason that where there are negative thought patterns then there must also be positive ones, based on the renewed mind that Heaven wants us to live from.

Keys

If the prison is our current location, then the keys could be understood to be the route out. The second part of the book will explore useful keys that can help us on our journey into greater freedom. I believe Father wants us to live in freedom and live with the right way of thinking, then there must be keys that can help us on this journey. I have learnt that, too often, we live as though there is no escape from the prison we find ourselves in. Perhaps we don't understand that the keys to those very prison doors are *already* in our hands! Alternatively, when we do have a sense that we have the keys in our hands, we often just don't seem to understand *how* to use them – we don't know how to appropriate the freedom that the use of the keys would give us. I will be showing you not just some keys, but also how to use them.

Palace

The final section of the book invites you to discover what it means to live in the palace. The palace is our destination. My prayer is that you will realise that even when you *feel* like you are back in the prison, you can still live from the palace, with a palace mindset. You will discover there are some steps you can take to live in that place of freedom, to live with a palace mentality, and how to keep your footing firmly in the palace, even though the events around you suggest otherwise.

We can be encouraged that the Bible is clear that we can overcome:

'Who is it that overcomes the world? Only he who believes that Jesus is the Son of God.'

1 John 5:5

If we are believers in Jesus, then we can be sure we have what is needed to overcome. Jesus has provided all that is required; we just need to learn how to take hold as our own that freedom that Jesus has already won for us by His blood. Since Jesus has accomplished this at the Cross, we need to understand and believe that this freedom is not just a future event for when He returns but is a reality we can – and should – experience now.

Paul teaches in his letter to the Galatians:

'It is for freedom that Christ ***has*** *set us free…'*

Galatians 5:1a (emphasis added)

Notice again the past tense: this is something already accomplished. It is not something that we might be able to attain to one day – Christ has done it; it is ours.

Jesus has set us free for a purpose. That purpose is simply that we live in freedom. If we are saved, then no matter how we feel, by nature we have been set free. We have already been set free from the prisons we find ourselves living in. We are free of shame, of guilt, and of fear. Because we are free, we are now free to experience all the joys of a relationship with Father God. We are now free to experience the love He has for us. If a prisoner is released from prison, he is no longer held by the bonds that once kept him locked up – he is set free. The past is just that: in the past. He can now look forward knowing he is free, without the restrictions of the prison. We are saved, we are set free from our past and from how we used to live life, and so there now are no restrictions for us because of all that Jesus has accomplished for us. The clothes the prisoner wore in prison are not the clothes he wears now. In the same way we now have new clothes ourselves. These are the robes of righteousness:

'I delight greatly in the LORD; my soul rejoices in my God. For he has clothed me with garments of salvation and arrayed me in robes of righteousness…'

Isaiah 61:10a

No matter how many times the enemy may come to accuse you, lie to you or remind you of something from your past, you can be sure of this: Jesus has made you clean. He has robed you with new robes. You have been made righteous (2 Corinthians 5:21). It is because of this fact that we can say we are righteous.

Also, we read:

'Now the Lord is Spirit, and where the Spirit of the Lord is, there is freedom.'

2 Corinthians 3:17

In fact, Paul continues to show us that not only are we made righteous because of the work of Jesus but also that He lives in us by the Holy Spirit. We read in First Corinthians:

'Do you not know that your body is a temple of the Holy Spirit, who is in you…?'

1 Corinthians 6:19a

Therefore, this leads us to understand that there is freedom for each one of us who is trapped in these prisons since we have the Holy Spirit, living inside of us, and this is because of the work of Jesus.

This is good news.

If it is, why do some of us live as though there is nothing we can do? Why do we live life as though there is no hope or no future? Why do we appear to have given up?

It may feel like there is no way out, but God **is** able to turn our situations around for good. Joseph in the Old Testament says:

'You intended to harm me, but God intended it for good to accomplish

what is now being done…'

Genesis 50:20

In Romans we read:

'And we know that in all things God works for the good of those who love him, who have been called according to his purpose.'

Romans 8:28

In both these verses there is hope and encouragement that whatever prison we find ourselves in, He is able to turn it around; we just need to press into Him. What the devil meant for harm, God can turn around for our good.

I want to encourage you that, as you continue to read the pages of this book, to believe that you can live a different life: a life of freedom, a life that Jesus made possible for each of us to live.

Part 1
Prison

Prison

What comes to mind when you think of prisons? Maybe you think of them as places for those who have done wrong or committed crimes – lockups for murderers, thieves or 'white collar' criminals.

There are different categories of prisons, from high security prisons for violent offenders considered a threat to society, to open prisons which may permit prisoners the possibility of day release.

No matter the category of prison, they all involve a degree of restriction and limitation. They involve captivity. They require monitoring of movement, restriction of visits, confinement, and the removal of liberty. There is no escape.

Do you sometimes feel like you are trapped? Do you feel like there is no way out? What do you feel your prison is? It might be an emotional or spiritual prison. Maybe your prison is shame.

Or perhaps fear… or disappointment? There are many types of prisons but no matter what they are, they all have one thing in common: they restrict, confine, and remove freedom. I'm sure that you, like I, have tried to escape many times - maybe with a temporary taste of freedom - only to find yourself back in the jail, confined once again.

Typically, a prisoner is sent to jail after being tried – and found guilty. Just like the prisoners locked away from society, we also might feel guilty, and as though some blame can be apportioned to us. However, it is also true to say that, unfortunately, there are times when miscarriages of justice send people to prison for crimes they did not commit. A wrongly convicted person still has the same restrictions as a guilty person: limits on freedom, no matter the real state of innocence.

If we feel that we are locked up in a prison, we need to understand and believe that we are judged 'not guilty'. It doesn't matter what the prison is, whether it is a prison of shame, fear, or a false sense of identity – Jesus has already paid the price for our release, and He has done what is required to obtain our freedom:

'For he has rescued us from the dominion of darkness and brought us into the kingdom of the Son he loves, in whom we have the redemption, the forgiveness of sins.'

Colossians 1:13-14

As a result of Jesus having rescued us and having paid the price for us, He does not see us as guilty. It doesn't matter how we see ourselves; the truth is that He no longer requires us to take the punishment of a guilty person. He has taken our sin and therefore, He looks at us and declares: "*Not Guilty*". We do not have to earn our way out of the prison we often find ourselves in. We do not have to do the time. The jailer (the devil) wants us to think we will serve a life sentence, with no chance of parole. Let's look at what Paul teaches in Romans:

'But now God has shown us a different way to heaven—not by "being good enough" and trying to keep his laws, but by a new way (though not new, really, for the Scriptures told about it long ago). Now God says he will accept and acquit us—declare us "not guilty"—if we trust Jesus Christ to take away our sins. And we all can be saved in this same way, by coming to Christ, no matter who we are or what we have been like. Yes, all have sinned; all fall short of God's glorious ideal; yet now God declares us "not guilty" of offending him if we trust in Jesus Christ, who in his kindness freely takes away our sins.'

Romans 3:22-24 (TLB)

If Jesus has paid the price for us and we are now 'not guilty,' why do we still live as though we are? Why do we still live as though we have to do the life sentence?

Our Guards

The prisons in our societies have guards in place to ensure that the inmates do not escape. We, too, may have guards in the prisons we find ourselves living in. Who are the guards that keep us locked up?

Often, the guard can depend on the type of prison. In the case of the prison of shame, for example, very often it is we who keep ourselves trapped. It doesn't matter how often someone else might say you are free; we continue to look back at what we have done and find ourselves unable to get free. In the case of the prison of disappointment, it is often those who have disappointed us who continue to entrap us. Whatever the prison, there often seems to be someone there guarding us and stopping us from opening the prison door and walking out.

We can also remain imprisoned by those detained with us. In other words, we can be influenced by those around us. Just as a prisoner who is jailed with other guilty people can succumb to or replicate the prison culture of 'survival of the fittest', we can begin to let the culture of those around us affect us for the worse, - even if we are not guilty. Soon, we find ourselves entrapped deeper. The deeper in the prison we are, the harder it appears for us to even try to escape.

Whoever the guards may be – ourselves or others – it doesn't matter until we realise the truth that the ultimate Head Guard is satan himself. He is the one who doesn't want us to escape. He is the one who would have us locked up for life. He is the one who wants to keep us in solitary confinement. He knows there is an escape route, but he does all he can to hide it from us.

Paul teaches us in Ephesians:

'For our struggle is not against flesh and blood, but against the rulers, against the authorities, against the powers of this dark world and against the spiritual forces of evil in the heavenly realms.'

Ephesians 6:12

I recently heard someone say that our battle is not against flesh and blood, but it often comes wrapped in it. So often we take out whatever frustrations we might have against the person who hurt us, the person who said the unkind words or the one who lied to us. But in truth we should remember it is the devil who is behind the shame or the fear that we feel. It is the devil who is ultimately the one keeping us trapped behind the prison walls and hiding the escape route from us.

I want to encourage you as you continue to read the chapters of this book to see that there *is* a way out. Shame is not your portion. Fear is not yours to carry. The prison you are in is *not* your home - you do not belong there. I want to encourage you that there are keys to your freedom and to use the keys you will find within this book. As you do, I pray that you will begin to experience freedom from these prisons and live as Jesus intended us to: a life living from the palace.

Lies

Have you ever watched a police drama in which the suspect is explaining things that he knows are a fabrication of events in order to convince the police that what he is saying is true? Similarly, in a court of law, the one giving testimony puts his hand on the bible and swears that he shall tell the truth, the whole truth and nothing but the truth. The intent is that the testimony which he will share will be completely reliable. It is then the job of the opposing counsel and the jury to distinguish any part of the story that doesn't ring true.

We understand the concept of truth and lies. We all hope that what people tell us is true, but there are times when we are told lies. These lies can be deliberate attempts to throw us off course or to make us believe something that simply is not true.

I am sure each of us would like to believe that we could see a lie for what it is. However, there can be times when our own experiences and thoughts inhibit us from seeing what is true. Thinking back to the crime dramas, how often has an investigation been slowed by the lead investigator being tricked into believing something to be true when we – the viewers – know it isn't? How often has their interpretation of the circumstances been clouded by their own thoughts or viewpoint, or maybe even pressure put on them by their bosses?

I had the privilege of living in Malawi for a number of years. Malawi is a country of two seasons: wet and dry. When it is the dry season, there is no rain. Without the rain, the countryside and vegetation begin to change colour to very brown and dry, and everywhere becomes dusty. However, when the rains begin everything changes, and the colour changes from brown to green. Everything looks alive again. Now, if you knew nothing about Malawi and visited in the dry season, no matter how much we insisted it's really a lush green landscape, you would be forgiven for thinking that the landscape always looked how you saw it: dry and dead. This goes to demonstrate that just because we believe something, it is not necessarily true and, equally, not believing something does not make it a lie.

We don't have to believe something for it to be true. Once, when I was leading a gentleman in a Sozo[2] session, he struggled to believe the truth of what God thought about him. Why? He had been believing a lie for so long that it was almost part of his DNA – he'd been thinking that what he believed about himself

---

[2] Sozo is an inner healing ministry developed by Bethel Church, Redding, California. The word Sozo is the Greek word that is used in the New Testament which means: Saved, Healed and Delivered.

was actually true. Even though God had shown him that it was a lie, his view had been so clouded by wrong thinking that he still found it difficult to believe the opposite. Just because he didn't really believe the truth, did that make it a lie? No! The truth was still true.

My wife used to say she didn't believe lies about God or, indeed, herself. However, when she had her first Sozo session many years ago she began to realise that she was believing lies about both God and herself. Often, we can be the same – we can believe lies as truth until one day it becomes clear that the thing we believed to be true is, in fact, a lie. A lie is perceived as truth until it is exposed.

Where do lies come from?

Let's have a look at a passage of scripture from the Gospel of John:

Jesus said to them, "If God were your Father, you would love me, for I came from God and now am here. I have not come on my own; but he sent me. Why is my language not clear to you? Because you are unable to hear what I say. You belong to your father, the devil, and you want to carry out your father's desire. He was a murderer from the beginning, not holding to the truth, for there is no truth in him. When he lies, he speaks his native language, for he is a liar and the father of lies. Yet because I tell you the truth you do not believe me…"'

John 8:42-45a

We see from these verses that Jesus is teaching us that lies come from the devil. Jesus says that the devil only knows how to speak lies. The Message version phrases it like this:

'When the liar speaks, he makes it up out of his lying nature and fills the world with lies.'

John 8:44b (The Message)

The devil is a liar, lies are the only language he speaks. It is in his nature to lie, he's the father of lies. It is impossible for him to tell the truth. He is the one who deceives us, and he's intentional about it. His lies are designed to confuse, deceive, and complicate our thoughts. Remember in the garden when the devil asked Eve: "*Did God really say…?*" (Genesis 3:1) He twisted what God had said to complicate and deceive Eve into thinking it was fine to eat of the fruit of the tree of knowledge of good and evil (Genesis 2:17).

We have seen that it is the very nature of the devil to lie. He can do nothing else and, he does all he can to hide that truth from us. Let us look at this same verse from the Passion Translation:

"'… He never stood with the truth, for he's full of nothing but lies – ***lying is his native tongue****. He is the master of deception and the father of lies!'"*

John 8:44b (TPT – emphasis added)

Whilst there are many countries that have English as their first language, there are many other countries that don't. For example, the French speak French, the Chinese speak Mandarin (on the whole), the main Kenyan language is Swahili, and so on. The languages of these countries are native to them. We see that the devil's native language is lying.

When my wife and I arrived in Malawi, we were unable to understand the language. We had learnt the basic greetings but, when people spoke anything else to us, it sounded like gibberish. The Chichewa language was not native to us. We had to learn it. The devil has not learnt any other language. It is foreign to him to tell the truth. The implications of believing his lies can be far reaching. Continually believing his lies limits us and hold us back. For example, take the lie "*I am worthless.*" We may have started to believe this lie through a negative experience, or perhaps been subject to someone repeatedly saying, "*You will never amount to anything.*" As a result, our thought patterns are framed in such a way that we don't think of ourselves the way that Father does, or we don't even think we are worthy to receive His love. We must learn to overcome the devil's lies with truth. The lies of the enemy are designed to keep us in prison.

When my wife and I taught in rural areas in Malawi, we needed a translator with us not only to translate what we said, but also what was being said to us. For our translator to be effective, she had to understand the context of the English we were speaking. It was no good the translator simply repeating what we had said word for word into Chichewa; she also needed to have an understanding of the subject matter. By understanding both the English language and the subject, our translator was effective in translating as she then used appropriate local examples of which we would have been unaware. When we had enough understanding of the local Malawian language, we had to then train our ears to hear what was being spoken. Once we accomplished this, we were more easily able to understand what was being said. Likewise, it's important for us to begin to identify when we are hearing the devil's native language, a lie, and recognise that it doesn't line up with the truth. When we expose a lie for what it is and reject it, this is another step on our journey into greater freedom and unlocking the prison door.

Jesus says:

"I am the way, the truth and the life…"

John 14:6

Jesus says that He is truth. He doesn't want us to listen to the lies of the enemy but, rather, listen to Him. He can be trusted. His words are to be believed. If we listen to Him, we can begin to understand the context of the lies that have been spoken to us, as He shines His light on them and begin to move from believing that lie to believing the truth.

We read in the temptation of Jesus (Luke 4:1-13) that He overcame the lies and temptations of the enemy with the Word. The enemy tried to use Jesus' circumstances to twist what Jesus knew to be true, to his own advantage, with the hope of causing Jesus to succumb to his temptations and lies. Three times the devil tempts Jesus around His hunger, His identity as the Son of God and, finally, Jesus' own suffering. Yet three times Jesus responds to the enemy: "It is written…."[3]

How often do we believe the words of the enemy over the words of Jesus? How often have we heard the lie of the enemy that says we are not loved instead of the truth that He lavishes His love on us? (1 John 3:1) A common lie we come across in Sozo sessions is the lie that we are not worthy and have no value,

---

[3] Luke 4:4. Luke 4:8 and Luke 4:10

instead of the truth which says we are His treasured possession (Deuteronomy 14:2). There are so many lies we can believe that simply are not true. The Bible is packed full of the truth that we can renew our minds with. I will look more closely at this and what it means in the chapter 'Renew our Minds'.

It is time that we allowed the Bible to translate the truth to us, rather than listening to the enemy, the liar.

The answer to being free from the lies is found in Jesus:

"If you hold to my teaching, you are really my disciples. Then you will know the truth, and the truth ***will set you free.****"*

John 8:31b-32 (emphasis added)

It is possible to know the truth. Jesus is the truth, and we can know Him. A truth is more than a piece of information that we process intellectually; it is an experience. It is something that is felt – a heart revelation. Jesus wants us to experience His truth, and with that comes freedom.

'For if you embrace the truth, it will ***release*** *true freedom into your lives.'*

John 8:32 (TPT - emphasis added)

When we embrace something, we hold it tightly and we willingly take hold of what is being said. Jesus wants us to hold tightly to the truth of what He says. Why? Because He knows that it will bring us into freedom. Jesus is truth - if we hold onto Him, He will release us into freedom. We are locked behind the prison doors of the lies we believe, but the keys to our freedom are found in the truth of the words of Jesus. The word '*release*' or "*set you free*" in John 8:32 is also translated delivered.[4] We are set free from the lies, we turn away from them and begin to live in the truth. When we allow His truth to become our reality, we can experience the freedom that He has already won for us on the cross.

How do we this?

When we have believed a lie for a long time, it is not always as easy as flicking a switch and suddenly, we believe the opposite, the truth. The lies may have taken root inside our hearts. As we have believed them for so long, it may feel like they still influence us.

So how do we overcome the lies?

I believe that, firstly, we need identify where the lie came from.[5] The lie is likely to have been spoken over you by someone else. If you're not sure where you first began to believe the lie, you could ask God to show you who you need to forgive in relation to the lie and to highlight what you need to forgive them for. It is important to forgive the person who spoke it over you. There is power in forgiveness and, by forgiving others, we are more able to come out of agreement with the lie.

Breaking agreement with the lie is the second thing I would encourage you to do. Just like in a legal agreement where two parties are agreeing to the terms, they are saying they will abide

---

4 https://www.blueletterbible.org/lexicon/g1659/niv/mgnt/0-1/ (accessed November 2022)

5 The following 3 steps are based on Bethel Sozo prayer tools.

by the document. This document then has the legal power over them. When we agree with something, we are effectively saying it is correct, which gives the thought we are agreeing with the power over our freedom. We have figuratively signed to say this is true, and we are thus held accountable to the agreement. Therefore, by coming out of agreement with it, we are saying that we no longer choose to believe it. In essence, we begin to rip up the legal document. We make a conscious decision to believe that what we are being told is not true, and we are saying that we want to have a different mindset. We no longer want that lie to have any control or influence over us. When we begin to come out of agreement with the lie, we begin to disempower its hold over us.

Thirdly, we need to ask Jesus what His truth is. As we begin to disempower the lie, we need to replace that lie with the truth. The lie "*I am worthless*" may be replaced with the truth that "*I am special*," "*I am worthy*," or "*I am valuable*." As we listen to the truth, the lie begins to have less authority in our lives. As the lie becomes weakened, we can begin to believe the truth and come into agreement with it. It may be a quiet voice at first but, as we continually align with this new truth, the voice will become louder until eventually the lie is drowned out and all we can hear is the truth of what Father thinks about us. We should begin to declare these truths. Say them out loud! Proverbs tell us:

'Your words are so powerful that they will kill or give life…,'

Proverbs 18:21a (TPT)

What we say has the power to bring either death or life. Consequently, the words we speak have considerable influence over us. What we speak also has consequences for the one speaking it. If, for example, we say we are worthless, we begin to believe that and, therefore, that lie then has the power to affect our attitudes to those around us and ultimately will keep us in bondage. Conversely, if we say we are special, the effect on us will be more likely to bring us into life – and into freedom.

As we continually declare these truths, the lie loses its power over us, and the truth can begin to take root in our hearts. As the truth become stronger in our lives, we can begin to walk in the newfound freedom that Jesus has for us.

Disappointment

I am sure we have all, at some time in our lives, experienced a level of disappointment. We have, no doubt, in some way or other, had feelings of being let down or of being hurt.

Disappointment happens when we experience an outcome that is different from that which we expected, or hoped for. That might come from another person when he or she doesn't meet our expectations. For example, a friend might promise to do something for you, but is then unable to fulfil that promise. Disappointment occurs after the negative action, or inaction, of something we had hoped would be either different, or positive. Whilst living in Malawi a friend promised he would do something, but this action did not materialise. I received no communication about the holdup and, as a result, I was left questioning what the problem was and felt a rising sense of distrust. This substantial let-down hurt my feelings and created disappointment with this person, whom I then felt I could no longer trust. Disappointment, when left unresolved leads to broken relationships.

Sometimes, disappointment might not involve another person; it might be that you are disappointed in yourself. When this happens, it can lead to feelings of shame, which we will look at in chapter 6. When this is the case, it's the result of you having an expectation of yourself that you couldn't live up to.

Sometimes, however, our disappointment is neither in others, nor in ourselves, but might be with God Himself.

Have you been asking God, for example, to heal a friend but the healing has not yet happened, and your friend is still sick? Or maybe you have been praying for a family member to come to know Jesus? Or perhaps you have a prophetic word that appears unfulfilled? When this happens, it is possible to be left feeling disappointed with God.

Many times when ministering inner healing to others, I have noticed that forgiveness is needed to be given, not only to friends or family members for disappointments experienced or felt, but also to God himself. To the disappointed person, initially, it might seem a little strange, or even theologically wrong, to need to forgive God, as He is perfect and, in truth, never lets us down. However, if we do indeed feel disappointment towards a situation that we were expecting God to move in, acknowledging this and actively forgiving Him for the disappointment will release us of the disappointment (and lack of trust) we might feel towards God. No matter who has disappointed us, it is important that we forgive.

I think it is important to understand the nature of disappointment. Disappointment happens when promises are broken or when something does not happen the way we think it should. Often, disappointment occurs when our perspective or understanding of an outcome is not fully met, or when the outcome is different to what we had expected. Sometimes, this is simply down to a miscommunication – we all have different life backgrounds and standards which affect our understanding and expectations; thus what one person says is very often different to what is heard by another. I am sure that when we were children, we played Chinese Whispers, the game in which each player whispers a message or phrase to the next player who, in turn, whispers what is heard to the next, and so on. By the time the sentence reaches the last person, what is heard and repeated aloud is very different to what was originally said at the start. It doesn't matter how many people are involved; sooner or later there will be a change in what is said and what is heard, through mishearing or lack of clarity. It is only when the original intent or phrase is revisited, that we can see where it 'went wrong'. Similarly, bringing disappointment or miscommunication into the open exposes it for what it is and permits a final readjustment to the understanding of the original intent.

Disappointment often starts out with the simple thought that it's a shame that the expectation wasn't met, or that it didn't turn out as it should have. However, as I have briefly mentioned, if this disappointment is left unchecked, it can fester and deteriorate. Likewise, with miscommunication between people, an unaddressed miscommunication, or even an unexplored disappointment in our own hearts, can become magnified or distorted. The more this happens, the more we will feel justified in our own interpretation of what happened and 'pass it on'. Just as in the game, each player passes on what he or she genuinely heard. The analogy for disappointment is the same - the person disappointed genuinely interprets the disappointment or miscommunication in a particular way. In doing so, we end up erecting barriers between ourselves and the one who hurt us. We feel validated in our thinking. We feel that we don't want to be let down and we don't want to go through that same disappointment. As this process continues, we can begin to develop an orphan mindset. An orphan mindset is essentially thinking which says, "*I am better on my own, I don't need the help of others.*" Ultimately, this may lead us to make a vow that says, "*I will never trust anyone again.*"

Feelings of disappointment will keep us looking at what hasn't happened, rather than looking at what God is doing. Our focus will be on the wrong thing. Ultimately, disappointment robs us of hope; disappointment, therefore, limits us. Whenever I have been let down by someone, I find myself looking at the action or inaction of whoever let me down which, in turn, moves my focus away from God and what He is doing.

We can all expect to go through disappointment at some point in our lives, but we should not let it govern how we live our life, nor let it rule us. Disappointment is not meant to define us; it is not meant to tie us up as if hostage to it.

The word appoint means to give or assign something to someone. The prefix "dis-" has its roots in the idea of: to be apart, or to be removed from.[6] Therefore, the problem with *dis-*

[6] https://www.twinkl.co.uk/teaching-wiki/dis-prefix (accessed July 2024)

appointment is that it separates us from our *appointment.* In other words, when we are *dis*-appointed, we become separated – or removed – from the very thing that was intended to be assigned to us, whether it be hope or trust etc. For example, if we have been let down, as with my example from when we lived in Malawi, then we begin to lose trust in the person who let us down, as the hoped for outcome did not materialise. Disappointment, therefore, robs us of the hope that should have been ours. When we have been robbed in this way, it can often remove any joy we may have and, in turn, may steal any happiness from us. Paul in his letter to the Romans says:

'And hope does not disappoint us, because God has poured out his love into our hearts by the Holy Spirit, whom he has given us.'

Romans 5:5

The Passion Translation renders this same verse:

'And this hope is not a disappointing fantasy, because we can now experience the endless love of God cascading into our hearts through the Holy Spirit who lives in us!'

Romans 5:5 (TPT)

We can see here that there is a link between hope and disappointment. Where there is hope, there is no disappointment. We can be encouraged, however, that if we have experienced disappointment, there is a solution, and the solution is – simply – God. He has poured out His unending love to us, and it never fails us. If something can never fail us, then it is impossible to be disappointed by it! Since God never fails us, we cannot be disappointed by Him. Therefore, we can put our hope in God.

You may be thinking that, earlier, I had suggested that people might have to forgive God for letting them down, failing them, or for the disappointment they feel towards Him. Yes, that is true, but if disappointment comes as a result of a miscommunication or a misunderstanding about an outcome, then often it simply stems from the outcome being different from what was expected or suggested initially. Let me give you a real-life example. Many years ago, my mum was ill in hospital, requiring a serious operation that the specialist and surgeons all agreed she was physically able to manage. After the operation, my mum appeared to be recovering when she developed a bleed on the brain; something no-one could have foreseen. Her body, already in a weakened state because of the operation, was now further compromised, which led to a life-threatening situation. I sought God for her, asking Him to work a miracle. It was then I felt God say to me, "*Your mum will be fine.*" I left the place of seeking Him and started thanking Him. It was about three days later we got a call to say that my mum was on life support, no longer breathing on her own, and that there was nothing else anyone could do. It was that day she died. Naturally, I was left with questions. Had God lied to me? Since we know that God is not a liar (Numbers 23:19, Titus 1:2), that did not seem like the answer; it simply could not be a possibility. Had I heard God correctly? Had I misheard Him? Yes, I was willing to accept I had not heard Him correctly, but something in my spirit could not agree that this was the case. If I *had* heard Him correctly, and if He is not a liar, then I was left with only one other outcome: simply, that my understanding of what God had said was different to His meaning. After seeking Him further on the subject, I concluded it was, indeed, that I had not understood His meaning. His perspective was that, as my mum was a believer, even death would not be the end. As a result, she was going to be fine, as He had said, since she was going to be with Him. My understanding had obviously been different; I heard what God said from my earthly standpoint of wanting to hear a certain way.

I could have allowed that situation to rob me. It could have caused me to be disappointed in God, *dis*appointing me – or removing me from the appointment I had with hope. Isaiah teaches:

'Then you will know that I am the LORD; those who hope in me will not be disappointed.'

Isaiah 49:23

Whenever we feel that God has let us down, whenever we feel disappointed by something God has not done, we should remember that God is not the cause of that disappointment; rather, it is our understanding of what He said, or our understanding of His timing. Let us remember:

'He is the Rock, his works are perfect, and all his ways are just. A faithful God who does no wrong, upright and just is he.'

Deuteronomy 32:4

Also:

'God, who has called you into fellowship with his Son Jesus Christ our

Lord, is faithful.'

1 Corinthians 1:9

We can trust Him completely. He is our rock; we can stand securely on Him. He is faithful – and that means that He is true to His word. It means He has integrity no matter the situation and will always do the right thing.

Overcoming disappointment

How, then, do we overcome such disappointment?

We should remember that disappointment is not a feeling we are designed for. We do not have to live with it. So, if we are experiencing it, we need to stop partnering with it. We can stop partnering with the lie that says we will always be let down. If we are believing that lie, then we need to ask Father what the truth is, and then begin to accept His truth as reality in our lives. If we have made a vow never to ask for help, we can ask God to forgive us for making that vow, and then start to reject the spirit of disappointment in our lives.

We need to recognise the nature of the disappointment by asking ourselves some questions. Where did it come from? Has it come from our expectation of another person? Has it caused us to no longer feel that we can trust this person specifically, or people generally? We need to extend forgiveness to the one who first let us down, causing feelings of disappointment. Forgiveness is the key to the beginning of freedom from many hurts. We don't necessarily need to tell the person who disappointed us about our forgiveness but, rather, simply choose in our hearts to forgive. We can then release the person from any judgements we have made about him or her, and resolve that the hurt and disappointment will not rob us anymore. It might be that this forgiveness and release is a process, requiring daily, repeated forgiveness, depending on the level of hurt caused.

It is quite likely that the people we need to forgive have no idea about how they have made us feel, especially when offences are simply down to misunderstandings, when it was never the intention to cause hurt in the first place, or when they have not considered the effects on us personally. In the example I gave at the beginning of the chapter from the episode in Malawi, after speaking to the person, I discovered that his vehicle had broken down and that he had run out of data on his phone, and was therefore unable to contact me to explain. It turned out that it was not his fault and that circumstances had been beyond his control.

Once we have started this journey of forgiveness for disappointments, we should pray. We can give how we are feeling to God. What does He have to say about what we are feeling? As we listen to Him, we can allow Him to give us His perspective on the situation. We let Him give us back what has been stolen from us. As we pray and seek His thoughts, we are then able to trust Him.

As I mentioned before, disappointment leads to distrust.

'Trust in the LORD with all your heart and lean not on your own understanding; in all your ways acknowledge him, and he will make your paths straight.'

Proverbs 3:5-6

As we begin to trust the Lord – or lean into Him and not our own thoughts or understanding – then we begin to recognise that we have His support. We do this by acknowledging Him, by listening to Him, and by getting to know Him. Being able to trust Him in the disappointment we may feel enables us to resist any attempts to have hope, happiness, or any other good thing, stolen from us.

God always hears us when we cry to Him:

'In my distress I called to the LORD; I cried to my God for help. From his temple he heard my voice; my cry came before him, into his ears.'

Psalm 18:6

Let's remember that hope does not disappoint (Romans 5:5). At the beginning of that same chapter, Paul gives us the reason for such a statement:

'Therefore, since we have been ***justified through faith,*** *we have* **peace with God** *through our Lord Jesus Christ, through whom we have* **gained access by faith** *into this grace in which we now stand. And we* **rejoice in the hope of the glory of God.***'*

Romans 5:1-2 (emphasis added)

If disappointment robs us of hope, then looking to Jesus will restore our hope. He is the reason for the hope that we experience. We have been justified by our faith in Him. Jesus has won that for us. This leads us to having peace with God. Peace is a foundation of our relationship with God, whether we feel it or not. Peace with Him is a fact. We are friends of God (John 15:15). In our relationship with God we receive and experience His grace. Everything which is His is also ours by grace. His power, His strength, His love. All this leads us to be able to rejoice in the hope we have in Him.

Jesus has made it possible for us to hope. He has overcome disappointment with hope. That which disappointment came to steal from us, Jesus has won back for us. Jesus is not just our hope. Jesus *is* hope.

Hopelessness

How often have you felt hopeless? How often have you felt like it was all for nothing? Maybe you have thought, "*What is the point?*" or maybe you have felt like giving up. What do your circumstances feel like right now? Does it feel like you just can't continue like you are? Perhaps it feels all too much, and you feel like you simply can't cope.

When we experience these thoughts and feelings, we often feel hopeless. We can feel like there is no hope of overcoming, or the breakthrough which we have been pursuing for so long feels so far away.

To hope is to have an anticipation of a positive outcome. Sometimes, however, when we talk about hope, there is an underlying sense of doubt, or an implication of, "*I wish….*" How many times have you either said to yourself, or heard someone else say, "*I hope so*" but really meaning, "*I am not convinced*"? Have you said, "*I hope it doesn't rain tomorrow,*" yet inside you are really thinking, "*I have no doubt it will rain tomorrow; I just don't want it to*!" When we use the word "hope", we have a sense of uncertainty, more like a wish than anything else. We use the word without any confidence.

However, biblical hope is the opposite. There is a certainty because is founded on God's nature and His promises to us.

Let's look at what the Bible says about hope:

'Hope does not disappoint us, because God has poured out his love into our hearts by the Holy Spirit, whom he has given us.'

Romans 5:5

We can count on hope in this verse because it is looking at what God has done. These words, "*Hope does not disappoint,*" provide comfort and reassurance. According to Paul, hope is more than a wish; there is a great sense of certainty and confidence. The Greek word *"elpis"* means a "favourable and confident expectation.[7]" It seems that hope, in this passage at, is something we can be sure of. No matter what we are hoping for from Him, we are not disappointed since God is to be trusted. When we put our hope in Him, there is no doubt – just trust. The word has a sense of anticipation to it rather than wishful thinking.[8] Therefore, based on our faith in who God is and His faithfulness, we can have a confident expectation in what we hope for.

---

[7]https://www.blueletterbible.org/search/dictionary/viewtopic.cfm?topic=VT0001404 (accessed July 2024)
[8]Nelson Study Bible, (1997) NKJV. Nashville: Thomas Nelson Publishers.

Where does hopelessness come from?

I think that sometimes hopelessness comes when we take our eyes off the One who *is* hope. When we feel hopeless, we have begun to look at the circumstances and begun to put our trust in what we can see, rather than the One who is unseen. The feeling of hopelessness comes when the situation we face seems bigger than the God of all hope. It is all too easy to focus on the problem.

When my wife and I were about to return to the UK on furlough from Malawi, the tenant in our British rental house gave us notice. At that time, the rental money formed a large portion of our income. Whilst in the UK, we were finding it hard to find a new tenant and, if things remained as they were, living without that income would have been very difficult. We attended a conference in Harrogate but, with the rental situation hanging over our heads, we were both finding it hard to focus on God – all we could see was our financial situation. One lunchtime, another delegate – whom we didn't know – told us that she had seen us with pound signs over our heads, and sensed that God was saying that finance would not be a problem. Remember, she knew nothing of our situation! That word encouraged and refocused us. That evening God got our attention. After the evening meeting we were hungry and went into a take-away restaurant to order just one burger, to share. As we entered, a member of staff said they were shut, but the other customers persuaded the staff to let us in. Happily, we gave our order and paid. Whilst we were waiting, the staff member said he had a spare burger and two portions of chips going to waste and asked if we wanted them for free. I felt God say to me this was a symbol of His provision. It seemed like it was an outworking of the word given to us earlier in the day. This unexpected blessing put our focus completely back onto Jesus. We no longer felt hopeless about our financial situation; we now had hope – the expectation that God was working. Sure enough, within a couple of weeks we had a new tenant in place!

The feeling of being hopeless doesn't mean that we have less hope; it means we feel that there is *no* hope. Therefore, when we feel hopeless, we feel we are without hope in the circumstance we are facing.

There **is** hope though. In those times when we feel like we are without hope, the Bible has some encouragement for us. Paul writes:

'May the God of hope fill you with all joy and peace as you trust in him, so that you may overflow with hope by the power of the Holy Spirit.'

Romans 15:13

Before we look at this verse more closely, let's also read what The Passion Translation says:

'Now may God, the inspiration and fountain of hope, fill you to overflowing with uncontainable joy and perfect peace as you trust in Him. And may the power of the Holy Spirit continually surround your life with his superabundance until you radiate with hope.'

Romans 15:13 (TPT)

As we read these two translations, it seems that there is a solution to feeling hopeless. The key is to trust in God. When we put our trust in Him, we are filled to overflowing with both joy and peace. When we feel hopeless, we lose our peace. Losing our peace leads us to losing our joy as well. Notice, however, that – as we trust Him – there is a promise that we will be filled once again with joy and with peace. Our joy and peace will return if we continue to believe Him. Paul says that joy and peace return to a point where they cannot be contained. As we put our focus back onto God rather than the circumstances around us, then He fills us. He is the answer. He is the solution. Paul then goes to show us that the outworking of that overflow of joy and peace is an abundance of hope. Notice that the NIV says: "*The God of hope.*" He is the author of hope. He is the personification of hope. Hope is found in a person – the person of Jesus, and not in anything else. Have you lost peace over a situation? Do you wake up in the morning dreading the day ahead? Focus on Jesus! Trust in Jesus because He is the inspiration of hope. As you do, then you will be surrounded by Him, and you will radiate hope once again.

If we have hope in Jesus, then we have a confidence and an expectation of Him. When we feel hopeless, we have taken our eyes off the One who gives us hope and in whom we can fully trust. If we are looking to Jesus, then we have no need to feel hopeless.

Faith and Hope

Faith and hope are two sides of the same coin. If we have faith, then we have hope.

Let's look at a verse in Hebrews:

'Now faith is being sure of what we hope for and certain of what we do not see.'

Hebrews 11:1

We can see from this verse there is a correlation between faith and hope. Faith gives us the certainty of that which we hope for. Faith says that despite my circumstances, I can still have hope.

If we look at this same verse in the NKJV, we get more of an understanding of what the writer is saying:

'Now faith is the ***substance*** *of things hoped for, the evidence of things not yet seen.'*

Hebrews 11:1 (NKJV emphasis added)

When reading this, we begin to understand that faith is a substance. In other words, faith is the reality of what we are hoping for. We could also put it like this: the things hoped for come into reality through faith. We get this same sense from The Passion Translation:

'Now faith brings our hopes into reality and becomes the foundation needed to acquire the things we long for. It is all the evidence required to prove what is still unseen.'

Hebrews 11:1 (TPT)

Our faith in God, trusting Him despite what we see around us, is the very thing that enables us to hope. Our faith is the basis of our hope. Without faith there is no hope. Faith causes our eyes to see what we can't see. It is clear in all three translations of this verse in Hebrews that, although we cannot see with our natural eyes, we can have hope. In fact, it is the testimony that is the basis of our faith, which enables us to see. Faith looks back. It says, *"It happened once, so it can happen again."* Hope is the expectation of the testimony of our past. It is because of our faith in God that we can hope.

If we can see what we hope for, then hope or faith is not required. Paul says in Romans:

'For in this hope we were saved. But hope that is seen is no hope at all. Who hopes for what he already has? But if we hope for what we do not yet have, we wait for it patiently.'

Romans 8:24-25

In essence, the hope we have – the hope in Jesus – is the expectation of a reality that is still to be seen.

When I was a child, I received pocket money each week. One week, my Dad said he was going to increase the value the following week. Faith said, "*I can trust my dad to fulfil what he said*," my experience was that my Dad kept his word, therefore I had something to look back on. The hope was the joy I felt with the expectation of what was to come.

In your current situation, what is it you need hope for? Maybe like in my story about the free burger, you are hoping for provision. Whatever the circumstance, whatever you need hope for, what does your history with God say? Let your testimony be the anchor point for your hope. Let your history be the hope of expectation for the future. As you look back on the testimonies of the past in this area, or if you currently don't have testimony of breakthrough in this area, let someone else's be your hope but, let those reminders of faith cause you to put your focus back on to God. As you do that, allow Him to fill you again with joy and peace, as promised, and then let that be the outworking of hope back into your life.

Shame

How many of us have experienced shame? How many of us look back at things we have done and feel guilty? We feel embarrassed, even humiliated, by an action in the past. How many of us feel ashamed, not so much what by *we* did, but by something that was done *to* us? Maybe we are embarrassed by the actions of someone close to us – a family member, perhaps – who did something that should not have been done? Have you ever tried to make someone else feel ashamed for something they did? Perhaps someone else has said, "*Shame on you*!" and you have agreed with those words.

Whatever situation resonates with you, if you have ever experienced these emotions (or maybe still do), you will know how they really make you feel. You will recognise the power that shame holds over your life. The enemy wants us to feel ashamed, and to continually look back at what we may have done with regret and guilt. He wants us to feel like there is no hope and that we really have blown it this time. He wants us to feel as though God really couldn't forgive us this time. Maybe we feel like satan is speaking suggestions in our ears such as, "*Do you remember that thing you did twenty years ago? You still remember it because God has not forgiven it.*" Or possibly he speaks words such as: "*You said to God last time that you'd never do that again, yet look – you did it again! There is no way to come back from this now.*" Perhaps he says things like, "*You deserve what that person did.*" A lot of us may have things in our lives we have felt shame about, or still do. Satan wants us to feel bad. He reminds us of our past to cause us to focus on what we did. He does this because he knows that when we repeatedly look at what we have done then we will feel ashamed. When we feel ashamed, we become too embarrassed to mention it. Then the more we hold shame in, the worse we feel – until eventually we feel like we could never be forgiven.

Look, however, at what Paul says at the reality we have in Jesus:

'Therefore, ***there is now no condemnation*** *for those who are in Christ Jesus.'*

Romans 8:1 (emphasis added)

Paul teaches "*now*," meaning at this very time. In other words, no matter when we read this verse, these words are true. In fact, Paul says it is better than that; he says that for those in Christ Jesus, the very moment we said yes to Jesus was the very moment that condemnation was no longer part of our lives. The word condemnation here means that a sentence is being pronounced. However, for those in Jesus, the sentence is: "*Not guilty*!" There is no sentence that can be pronounced against us. Shame says we are guilty, but Jesus says that we are innocent of all charges.

His grace **is** sufficient for us (2 Corinthians 12:9). If Jesus says there are no charges against us, why do we listen repeatedly to the lying tongue of the enemy which says otherwise? The truth is that shame feels so strong and so real. If we expose ourselves, if we let others in on the secret, then we will feel even worse – perhaps that our life is over. Shame leads to condemnation. Shame says: "*You are guilty.*"

Let's take a moment to look at the same verse, from The Passion Translation:

'So ***now the case is closed****. There remains* ***no accusing voice of condemnation*** *against those who are joined in life-union with Jesus, the Anointed One.'*

Romans 8:1 (TPT – emphasis added)

This is really good news!

It is important to point out two things: firstly, God turns to us and says: "*The case is closed; you are free to go.*" Secondly, every time the enemy tries to bring us against the judge of Heaven, it is like God is saying to the accuser, "*I can't hear the accusation. I have already ruled on this.*" You see, there is no voice against us.

Let's take a moment to look at where shame came from:

'When the woman saw that the fruit of the tree was good for food and pleasing to the eye, and also desirable for gaining wisdom, she took some and ate it. She also gave some to her husband, who was with her. And he ate it. Then the eyes of both of them were opened and they realised that

they were both naked; so they sewed fig leaves together and made coverings for themselves.'

Genesis 3:6-7

Right at the very beginning, it appears that shame came upon us. Notice that Adam and Eve ate of the fruit of the tree of knowledge of good and evil and, as they did so, their eyes were opened. What was the first thing they observe? They realise they are naked. Their shame was real at that very moment. Adam and Eve appear, at that point, to feel guilty; they now feel shame. It is worth remembering that it was not the act of eating the fruit that caused them to be naked – it simply caused them to realise that they were *already* naked. Adam and Eve were naked before they ate the fruit, yet they were not ashamed.

Notice in the earlier chapter:

'The man and his wife were both naked, and they felt no shame.'

Genesis 2:25

It seems clear that mankind was not created with shame; shame came upon us when they listened to the snake (satan). How Adam and Eve now saw themselves changed from the moment they realised their vulnerability. Shame causes us to feel vulnerable.

It is worth noting that Adam and Eve covered themselves by using plants to conceal their nakedness. They were embarrassed so they tried to hide their shame from each other.

We read just a few verses later:

'Then the man and his wife heard the sound of the Lord God as he was walking in the garden in the cool of the day, and they hid from the Lord among the trees of the garden.'

Genesis 3:8

Not only did Adam and Eve try to hide from each other, they also tried to hide from God Himself. Adam and Eve had covered themselves, but their own efforts didn't amount to anything. Since the coverings they used were inadequate, they still felt embarrassed at the state of their nakedness – so much so that they even felt the need to hide from God.

Shame leads us to hide! Shame causes us to run away. Shame controls us. When we feel shame, we strive to avoid exposure.

If we end the story there, we might think that our own futile efforts are all we have. We might think I know the shame I feel, and the compulsion to try to hide that shame. If only I can continue to put a brave face on it, I might just get by… Maybe no one will notice the shame I am carrying around….

The story doesn't end there! We read in the next few verses:

'But the Lord God called to the man, "Where are you?"
He answered, "I heard you were in the garden, and I was afraid because I was naked; so I hid." And he said, "Who told you that you were naked? Have you eaten from the tree from which I commanded you not to eat?"'

Genesis 3:9-11

God enters the garden, as He always did. He was looking for an intimate conversation with Adam and Eve, yet this time something was different. They were hiding. God did not say; "*What have you done?*" There is no hint of blame or accusation from God. God continued to love Adam and Eve. In God's question, "*Where are you?*" it is He who wants Adam and Eve first to recognise where they are, and then to recognise what they have done. God wanted Adam and Eve to come out of hiding and to be open with Him. It is only then that God can start to rebuild the brokenness that both Adam and Eve felt. It is only when they admit their mistake that the intimacy that God desired to have with them is restored. How did God begin to restore Adam and Eve?

'The Lord God made garments of skin for Adam and his wife and clothed them.'

Genesis 3:21

It took God to clothe Adam and Eve since they had made an ineffective effort to cover their shame. God was able to redeem their nakedness and shame. Only when Adam and Eve admit their shame is God able to clothe them and cover their shame.

The Bible tells us that when Jesus was crucified, He was stripped naked, and His clothes divided (Mark 15:24). As He hung on the cross, He was ridiculed (Mark 15:29) and mocked (Mark 15:31). Jesus was covered in shame. Jesus went through this most humiliating act in order to cover our shame. In fact, when we read Isaiah, we get a better picture:

'For he has clothed me with garments of salvation and arrayed me in a robe of righteousness, as a bridegroom adorns his head like a priest, and as a bride adorns herself with her jewels.'

Isaiah 61:10

Jesus has dealt with any shame we may feel by removing that shame and clothing us with new garments of righteousness. These garments are likened to those worn by a bride and groom; each of whom dresses in his or her finery. Nowadays, the bride will usually be dressed in a beautiful white wedding dress. White normally represents purity and innocence. The robes of righteousness that Jesus clothes us in are of purity and innocence therefore, we are free from the guilt of shame and condemnation.

Let's take a moment to look at a couple of stories from the Gospel of John to see how Jesus responds to the two people who, in the world's eyes, should be covered in shame.

The first story is the conversation between Jesus and a Samaritan woman at the well (John 4:5-30):

Jesus said, "Go get your husband and bring him back here." "But I'm not married," the woman answered. "That's true," Jesus said, "for you've been married five times and now you're living with a man who is not your husband. You have told the truth."'

John 4:16-18 (TPT)

Have you noticed that the woman was at the well in the hottest part of the day (John 4:6), when no-one else would be around?

Her reputation would have gone before her, causing people to shun her, according to their culture. In addition to this, the conversation Jesus has with her is not normal, as a Jewish man would not ordinarily be speaking to a Samaritan woman, and especially not with a woman of poor moral character.

We see that Jesus neither condemns her nor makes her feel embarrassed at the truth. While there is no-one else around, He gently and lovingly enables her to stop hiding in her shame – so much so that at the end of their interaction, she goes back home to tell everyone about the conversation:

'Come and meet a man at the well who told me everything I've ever done!'
John 4:29a (TPT)

This woman had been infamous for how she lived her life. Nevertheless, her public testimony and honest confession following her conversation with Jesus demonstrate that she was now ready to step out of the garment of shame she had been wearing and put on the garment of righteousness that Jesus was offering her. Had Jesus heaped condemnation on her, she would have wanted to continue to hide and live her life as before. However, she was now free – shame had lost its power over the woman.

The second story is that of the woman caught in adultery (John 8:1-11):

'… "If any of you is without sin, let him be the first to throw a stone at her." Again he stooped down and wrote on the ground. At this, those who heard began to go away one at a time, the older ones first, until only Jesus was left with, the woman still standing there.

Jesus straightened up and asked her, "Woman, where are they? Has no-one condemned you?" "No-one sir," she said.
"Then neither do I condemn you," Jesus declared. "Go now and leave your life of sin."'

John 8:7b-11

The woman was being brought to Jesus, full of shame. She was guilty of that which she was being accused. Jesus' response, however, was very different to that of those accusing her. His is one of humility (He stoops down) and gentleness. Once again, before He addresses her situation, He ensures there is no-one else in earshot. He does this because He knows shame is overcome in the secret place and doesn't need to be called out publicly. Shame hides and therefore, we are set free from its effects in the quiet, private place.

I once led a day conference on the Father Heart of God, where I sensed God was highlighting to me that some people present were experiencing shame. I felt there were a number of people whom Jesus wanted to set free from shame. Instead of asking those who felt shame to stand, I asked *every* person in the room to stand so that more shame would not be heaped on those who already struggled under it. Shame is bad enough without being ashamed of the shame that we carry! I encouraged every person in the room to prophetically take off the cloak of shame they were carrying and throw it to Jesus. I then led everyone to put on the new robes that Jesus was giving in its place. About a week later, someone thanked me for how I had led that ministry time in relation to shame. The person had been struck by how I involved everyone and not just those who felt they carried shame. He found that very powerful and said it would stay with him forever. I tell this story simply to illustrate that shame is broken off with love, gentleness, and humility.

Paul teaches us in Romans:

'As the scripture says, "Anyone who trusts in him will never be put to shame."'

Romans 10:11

If we trust in Jesus, we do not need to carry shame. It is only the enemy who wants to keep us bound up in shame because he wants us to continually look back at the things we have done, or have had done to us. However, there is hope. There is freedom. Jesus is the answer to shame. It requires us to have faith and be humble enough to admit any wrongdoing on our part. Just as Adam and Eve were humble, as was the Samaritan woman, but in both cases shame was met with the same humility, it was met with love and gentleness.

No matter where we are in relation to shame, it is possible to escape the hold it has over our lives. My wife and I were ministering to a lady who for decades had been carrying the shame of something that had been said about her by someone else. She had been battling feelings of shame and other feelings that came with it for so long that it was as though shame was part of who she was. She saw no way out. As we ministered, Jesus revealed the first time these shameful feelings had come upon her and she was then able to release forgiveness to the person involved. She heard what Jesus had to say, what He thought about her and, as she began to accept Jesus' truth, she suddenly began to cry. In that moment, something shifted – it was like shame literally left the room and the lady felt lighter and happier. It was evident that she was no longer covered in shame.

No matter how you started to feel shame, there is freedom! It might be that you need to forgive someone, or reject any lie that you are believing about yourself or the situation. You can then ask Jesus to replace that lie with His truth and, as you begin to accept that truth, begin to walk in the freedom that Jesus offers, as if "*not guilty*" is true of you.

Fear

We all understand fear. We know what it is to experience fear. Fear and anxiety are prevalent in society today. There are different types of fear; fear of spiders, fear of heights, or fear of water are some examples. Other fears could include a fear of failure, fear of being alone, fear of death, or fear of the future. The first list is a list of things that are external to us. The second list are more internal fears. Both are as genuine as the other. No matter how small or big the fear or phobia is, the feeling of fear is real.

Whatever the fear is, there will have been a cause to experiencing the fear. Have you ever heard someone ask "*Why do you fear spiders? They won't harm you*". This kind of question, although well-meaning, doesn't help the person who has a fear of spiders. Whatever the fear is - it has come from somewhere. You were not born with that fear. Take my mum for example; she had a fear of water. When she was a young girl, she was taught to swim. When she was learning in the sea a wave came over her and she briefly went underwater. It was the moment of going under that caused her to fear water. It was easy to pinpoint when her fear of water started. Sometimes, however, these fears can creep up on us over time; they are unconsciously received. I'm sure none of us who have experienced fear have actively thought, "*If only I could fear…*". The point is the fear we face, originated from somewhere. Something happened, or something was said, that caused that fear to rise up within us.

My wife and I had the privilege of ministering to a lady who had a fear of heights. As we started, we asked the lady if there was anyone she needed to forgive in relation to this fear. It transpired that when she was a young girl her Dad had taken her to a high tower. Whilst admiring the view from the top her Dad playfully pretended to push her. The father never intended to harm his little girl, and certainly not push her from that tower. It was at this point the father should have explained to the little girl that he was playing and reassured her she was safe. But what had happened in that innocent playing time was that the little girl, who did not understand, had subconsciously learned that heights are unsafe. As a result, instead of enjoying playing with her dad, she grew up with a real fear of heights. As we led her through a simple process of forgiving her dad, and hearing what Jesus said to her about the fear - she became free of that fear of heights.

I know someone who had a fear of butterflies. This fear was genuine for her. Whenever she saw a butterfly, or a butterfly flew anywhere near her, she would freeze on the spot. It was a knee-jerk reaction which she couldn't control. The fear was so real that it felt like she couldn't move. Often the fears we face stop us from moving forward; they hold us back and can literally paralyse us.

The enemy wants each of us to live in fear, because as we do, we are more likely to stand still – it becomes harder to move forward in our God given destiny. We can become a prisoner to that fear. For example, if someone has a fear of speaking in public, they are unlikely to stand up in public and share a testimony of something God has done. The fear that prevents the testimony being shared may deny someone else being encouraged by the testimony.

Let's take a look at some Bible verses that relate to fear. Firstly:

'There is no fear in love. But perfect love drives out fear, because fear has to do with punishment. The one who fears is not made in perfect love.'

1 John 4:18

The lady I mentioned who had a fear of heights in that moment was experiencing fear, not love, when her Dad was pretending to push her at the top of the tower. Remember - the Dad had no intention of causing his daughter to have a fear of heights, to him they were just playing. To her however, this was the moment fear entered her life. We learn from this verse that perfect love casts out fear. We know that God is love (1 John 4:8). If God is love, it is possible for us to live without fear. If we live in God, who is love, there does not need to be fear.

The New King James says:

'There is no fear in love; but perfect love casts out fear, because fear involves ***torment.****'*

1 John 4:18 (NKJV - emphasis added)

The word used in the New International Version for punishment is replaced in this translation with the word 'torment'. Someone who is in torment could be said to be agonising over something. Torment can also refer to suffering. When we fear we suffer. Love and safety go hand in hand. When we feel loved, we also feel safe. If we feel like we are suffering, or being punished, we often lose our sense of safety. Why do some children have comfort blankets? To make them feel safe, and often to make them feel protected from something they fear. Jesus is the One who comforts us; He becomes our blanket of love and safety.

This perfect love gives us no room for fear. It *is* possible to feel completely safe. Jesus is the personification of perfect love. It is Jesus who casts out fear. Jesus replaces our fear with Himself - love. There is an invitation to be so hidden in His love in order that fear cannot survive. The Passion Translation says: "*Love never brings fear.*" (1 John 4:18a). His love *is* the antidote to fear!

Secondly, the Bible teaches faith and fear should not co-exist. Let's take a look at a story where the disciples experienced fear, and Jesus' response:

'Without warning, a furious storm came up on the lake, so that the waves swept over the boat. But Jesus was sleeping. The disciples went and woke him saying, "Lord save us! We're going to drown!" He replied, "You of

little faith, why are you so afraid?" Then he got up and rebuked the winds and the waves, and it was completely calm.'

Matthew 8:24-26

I can picture the disciples panicked and worried - I can almost hear the fear in their voices as they wake Jesus up. The disciples thought they were going to drown, they feared for their lives. As their fear kicked in; their only hope was Jesus.

Jesus' response is an interesting one. He is woken by His disciples. He hears their fear. He knows what they are afraid of. However, He firstly addresses *them* and not the storm itself which was causing the disciples to feel fearful. Jesus had no problem with the storm. His concern was primarily that His disciples had taken their eyes off Him. They were looking at the storm and not at Him. Jesus firstly wants to bring the disciple's focus back onto Him; the One who can calm the storm. When we face fears, no matter what they may be, the answer is always to look to Jesus. The fear will always appear larger than it is. Fear looks at the circumstances. Faith looks to Jesus. Fear takes our attention off Jesus; it alters our perspective.

Jesus is not rebuking the disciples for their lack of faith; He is reminding them that looking to Him dispels the fear. He knows that when we continue to look to Him, our trust will remain in Him. It is impossible to be fearful and have faith. It is like hot and cold; they are opposites. Fear is simply trusting something that cannot be trusted. Fear cannot be trusted! However - Jesus can be trusted! When we trust Jesus, we are not going to partner with fear and allow it to define us. We allow Jesus - and Jesus alone - to define us.

I will look in later chapters at ways we can close the door to fear in our lives.

Thirdly, the Psalmist has some comforting words for us that will encourage us to keep our eyes on Him:

'I sought the LORD, and he heard me, And delivered me from all my fears. They looked to him and were radiant…'

Psalm 34:4-5a (NKJV)

If we seek Him, look what happens – we are delivered from our fears. The word 'delivered' here means to snatch away;[9] the sense is being snatched by force. The fear is forcibly removed from us. Where fear may have a grip on us, even a tight grip - when we look to Him and place our trust in Him, then fear loses its grip and is forcibly removed. There is nothing fear can do at this point. If the grip was still there when the fear was removed there would be a scar, but we can be sure with Jesus there are no scars of fear left - there is no residue remaining. Notice, when we seek Him, that we are delivered from **all** fears; we look to Him and are radiant. The Hebrew word for radiant is "*nahar*" which means "to sparkle" or be "cheerful."[10] The Psalmist is saying that without fear we are more cheerful and lighter in ourselves.

I mentioned earlier in this chapter about the lady with a fear of butterflies. As my wife and I ministered with her she had a vision

---

[9] https://www.blueletterbible.org/lexicon/h5337/kjv/wlc/0-1/ (Accessed November 2022)
[10] https://www.blueletterbible.org/lexicon/h5102/niv/wlc/0-1/ (Accessed November 2022)

where Father had a butterfly on His finger. He lovingly and gently offered her His finger for her to first stroke the butterfly. Only after the lady was comfortable, did He offer her to have the butterfly land on her finger. Notice how kind and gentle Father was; He didn't suggest the young lady was silly to have such a fear. He saw her, He recognised the fear, and slowly, at her pace released the influence this fear had on her. As the fear was removed, she entered into freedom. When we had finished ministering to her there was a difference in her appearance - there was a sparkle in her eyes, and she had a smile on her face. (Interestingly, I have since heard that she now feels safe to physically have butterflies land on her finger.) What a beautiful picture of someone looking to Jesus, and the fear being snatched away from her to the point where she is now able to sparkle.

We've seen by focusing our eyes on Jesus and living in His love dispels fear – we've also seen that when fear is gone, we can sparkle.

Finally, let's look at another verse to encourage us to keep our focus on God and remain in His perfect love:

'So do not fear, for I am with you; do not be dismayed, for I am your God.'

Isaiah 41:10

What an amazing promise. God is promising to be with us as our God. He is reminding us that we can trust Him. He is showing us that if He is with us, then there is nothing to fear. Let's imagine a child who fears that monsters are under their bed. What loving parent wouldn't come and comfort their child and sit with the child until they were once again asleep? Parents want their children to feel safe. God is reminding us that He is a good and perfect Father. He is with us, and we are safe with Him. He loves us - there is therefore nothing to fear. Paul declares in Romans:

'For you did not receive a spirit that makes you a slave again to fear, but you received the Spirit of sonship.'

Romans 8:15

What an amazing verse - full of hope! We don't have to fear - we have received the Spirit of sonship! We have received the Holy Spirit who lives inside of us and as a result fear no longer has to be a part of our lives - fear no longer has to influence us.

Just like the lady with the fear of butterflies, the fear had a hold on her in that part of her - she was a slave to it. How did the lady become free? As is often the case when my wife and I are ministering to people with fear, the lady first asked Father where the fear came from; remember we are not born with fear. She remembered a time when she was young and that something had happened; she then asked Father to show her where He was in that moment.[11] Father showed her that He was with her and how close to her He was. It was at this moment that fear began to lose its grip on her. The young lady saw that Father was with her, it was then that she felt loved by Him, and she felt safe once again. She had refocused her eyes on Him and not the fear. The lady had spent twenty years affected by this fear of butterflies, it

---

[11] This is a tool called 'Presenting Jesus' used in Bethel Sozo.

had control over her, and in no more than forty-five minutes she was no longer a slave to it - she was free!

I was recently talking to this same lady. She told me how she sometimes has to remind herself of her vision from Father where she allowed the butterfly to land on her finger. There are times when we must walk in the new-found freedom Father gives us. When we have been locked up for so long it is easy to revert to that old way of thinking. When fear has been a part of our lives for so long it is a conscious choice to declare *'I no longer partner with that fear, it is no longer part of my life, and I am no longer a slave to fear'*. This lady remains completely and wonderfully free; she makes a regular decision, however, to partner with the new freedom she now enjoys.

Rejection

Many of us, either now or in the past, have experienced feelings of rejection. Rejection, simply put, is when we don't feel wanted or accepted. These feelings can develop over time, when maybe time and again we were either laughed at for something we did, picked last for a sports team, or we felt ignored and not listened to. Sometimes, however, these feelings are experienced in an instant; for example, becoming aware of our marriage partner being unfaithful.

If rejection is something you often feel, then the influence of social media can easily intensify those feelings – for example by someone not liking or commenting on a post. We begin to take it personally that our post was ignored and we can feel even more rejected. I have ministered to many people who have been affected deeply by rejection - so much so that the feeling has become familiar to them, and consequently they filter every response through rejection. They expect to be rejected and look for it in the responses of others.

No matter the level of rejection we encounter, the fruit is always the same. Hurt. The rejection we feel hurts more because it involves relationships and relationships matter to us. Rejection is very often caused by broken relationships, either the ending of a broken relationship or the words that are spoken which cause the relationship breakdown.

The pain of rejection that we feel is real and is hurtful. Scientists have discovered that the part of the brain that is activated when we experience physical pain is the same part of the brain that is activated when we feel rejected.[12] So if you were to fall over, for example, and break a limb, the pain felt is in the same part of the brain as when you feel rejected; albeit an emotional pain rather than a physical one.

Someone who experiences rejection may also, at some point, experience feelings of shame, guilt or loneliness. They may begin to feel that everyone is against them. Another side effect of rejection can be jealousy. Jealousy can begin to develop in a person feeling rejected because they may feel that someone values our relationship or what we have to say, less so than someone else.

Over time, if these feelings of rejection are left unresolved, the thoughts we have about ourselves become inward-looking. We begin to isolate ourselves from others; after all, *I've been rejected*

---

[12]https://ideas.ted.com/why-rejection-hurts-so-much-and-what-to-do-about-it/ (accessed January 2024)

once, what is stopping others from treating me in the same way? Our sense of self-worth begins to diminish because, clearly, *I'm not likeable or loveable. People don't want to be around me.* Our self-esteem might be affected; we feel as though we aren't good enough to be around others. Ultimately, someone suffering from rejection can feel unloved.

We all want to be loved and accepted. Each of us has an innate desire to belong – if we don't feel like we belong, we feel rejected. We may value ourselves by how much we feel we belong and are accepted. Therefore, when our sense of belonging begins to be questioned, we react negatively to what people say or how they act around us.

People who regularly feel rejected may begin to act in a particular way to make themselves more attractive to others, so that in turn they begin to feel wanted and accepted. However, by doing this, people are putting on a mask over who they really are. The problem with this kind of behaviour is that the rejected person becomes tired and eventually the mask slips. People begin to see underneath the mask, which results in the rejection they have tried so hard to hide from others, being triggered. When left unhealed it can only take a small trigger before a greater reaction occurs and the rejected person feels angry and hurt. This can lead to a cycle - the person on the receiving end of our anger begins to pull away, leaving the rejected person feeling validated in their rejection, and so the mask becomes even more firmly in place.

As this cycle continues, we can unintentionally, or even intentionally, put up walls around our hearts to protect ourselves from being hurt. We want to keep people out. We want to ensure we don't suffer any more hurt and rejection. There are, however, twofold effects to erecting such a wall. Firstly, they become successful in keeping others at a distance, which in turn leads us to feel as though we don't belong. This extenuates our feelings all the more. Secondly, as Christians, the wall also keeps God away from our heart. Whilst the wall has the effect of protecting ourselves from others, we have erected a barrier between ourselves and God and therefore find it more difficult to feel His love and acceptance. I've had the privilege of ministering to people who have put up a wall of protection[13] and it's always wonderful to see people set free as their wall comes down. When this has been the case, I have found it helpful to ask the person if there is anyone they need to forgive. Forgiveness is a key to the wall coming down.

If we have put a wall up around our heart to protect it, we are placing our trust in the wrong thing. We're in essence saying *'I can protect myself; I will be ok if I stay behind my wall.'* The truth is that we can't protect ourselves. When we try to protect ourselves however, invariably we end up just hurting ourselves. Father God is the One who wants to protect us. He loves us unconditionally and He is the one who wants to show us our real value.

God created us in His image (Genesis 1:27) which means that just as God loves and feels loved, so can we. If we have an in-built desire to be loved and valued, then keeping others out by erecting a wall enhances any rejection we feel. Therefore, we also find it hard to experience intimacy, not just with our earthly relationships, such as friends and family, but also with God. God

---

[13] Taken from a Bethel Sozo prayer tool.

is a Father who desires intimacy with His children. He is the One who wants to be close to us and for us to feel close to Him.

We read in Paul's first letter to the church in Corinth:

'But whoever is **united** *with the Lord is* **one** *with Him in spirit.'*

1 Corinthians 6:17 (emphasis added)

The Greek word for united is *'Kollao'* which means to be glued together or to be fastened firmly. It can also mean cleaved to.[14] This word is the same as the Hebrew word *'dabaq'* used in Genesis 2 referring to a husband and wife.

'That is why a man leaves his father and mother and is **united** *to his wife, and they become* **one** *flesh.'*

Genesis 2:24 (emphasis added)

I'm sure we can all understand this, even if we have not experienced the intimate relationship of a husband and wife. Paul is saying the relationship God wants with each of us is a relationship with the same level of intimacy. Just as a husband and wife are glued together, so He wants us to be glued to Him. How can there be intimacy if there is a wall or barrier between two people? The effect of this intimate union, as we have seen in both passages is to be one; to be in complete union or fully committed to each other. Each part is inseparable from one

[14] https://www.blueletterbible.org/lexicon/g2853/niv/mgnt/0-1/ (accessed January 2024)

another. We are literally one. If there is a wall, the desired intimacy is broken.

We saw earlier that human desire is to be loved and wanted, and often we base our self-worth from how people interact with us. However, the problem is that our value is coming from the wrong place. When we feel rejected and begin to push people away, we put that wall up which contradicts the heart of God that says we are loved and valued. He created us and He knows our need for value - we were created to receive our value from Him. The rejection we feel is because we place a higher value on our earthly relationships and how we are seen by people, as opposed to how God feels about us.

Let's have a look at this theme in the Bible:

'Be strong and courageous. Do not be afraid or terrified because of them, for the Lord your God goes with you; he will never leave you nor forsake you.'

Deuteronomy 31:6

What comforting words. If rejection is the feeling of being abandoned and forsaken, then God is clearly stating He never rejects us.

The writer of Hebrews reminds us of this same promise:

'I will never leave you alone, never! And I will not loosen my grip on your life!'

Hebrews 13:5b (TPT)

God is saying He will *never* desert us; He will *not* loosen His grip on us. Simply put - God is by our side for the entirety of our life. When it feels like others have deserted us, God will never desert us. He continually holds us in His hands.

When we read this verse in the Amplified version, we get a deeper understanding of what the writer is conveying:

'...for He has said, "I will never [under any circumstances] desert you [nor give you up nor leave you without support, nor will I in any degree leave you helpless], nor will I forsake or *let you down* or *relax My hold on you [assuredly not]!'*

Hebrews 13:5b (AMP)

The truth of God never leaving us clearly comes across in this translation. We read there is nothing that will cause Him to leave us. In fact, nothing will ever compel or move Him to leave us or give up on us. There is nothing that we can do that would make Him abandon us. If this is the case, we should never feel rejected or abandoned by God. If ever we feel abandoned by God, I suggest that it is us who have moved away from Him. It is never the other way around.

We read in Psalms:

'For the LORD will not **reject** *his people; he will never forsake his inheritance.'*

Psalm 94:14 (emphasis added)

The word 'reject' here also means abandon, forsake, or let go of.[15] What a wonderful, freeing verse! We see from these verses that God is not capable of rejecting us. He will not leave us or desert us. He will never let go of us. There is nothing that will even make Him think about it. He will remain faithful to us (1 Thessalonians 5:24). If we are believers in Him then He is by our side forever; He will hold us and keep us close.

Earlier we saw that when we feel rejected by people, we might feel that everyone is against us - but let's have a look at this verse in Romans:

'What, then, shall we say in response to these things? If God is for us, who can be against us?'

Romans 8:31

The verses we have looked at, and many others in Scripture, help us know the truth that rejection is never part of God's plan for us. However, the enemy has other plans. Satan wants us to feel locked in the prison of rejection because in this prison we feel alone and abandoned. In this prison we find it difficult to believe the truth of who we really are. As I explained earlier, these feelings are self-perpetuating. When we are within the walls of the prison of rejection, we feel even more justified in our thoughts, and so the feelings deepen. This continuing cycle makes it difficult for us to believe that God will never leave us. When we are in this prison it can feel like nothing can penetrate

---

15 https://www.blueletterbible.org/lexicon/h5203/niv/wlc/0-1/ (accessed January 2024)

the walls; that there is no escape route. The prison of rejection can often feel one of the darkest.

How then, can we begin to leave this prison? How can we find freedom and begin to truly experience what we have seen God says in His word; but also feel the love the Father has for us?

I mentioned earlier in this chapter that forgiveness is important, as it is with many of the prisons mentioned in this book. (In the second part of this book, I will look at forgiveness in more depth). The feelings of rejection will have started somewhere, whether it be slowly and subtly, or more obviously - but a situation or a person will have started it. Remember - we were not designed to feel alone nor were we created to partner with feelings of rejection. God created us to be in union with Him and others - so ask Him to show you who you need to forgive. You might be surprised at the answer, but I would encourage you to forgive. No matter how hard it might be, just starting the journey of forgiveness will begin to unlock the prison door of rejection.

Also, depending on how the rejection started, you might ask Jesus to show you where He was with you at that time. Again, remember that He never leaves us, therefore He was somewhere nearby. Ask Him to show you how He felt about the situation. In these painful memories it's powerful to see where Jesus was and begin to understand how He felt about it. After all, the Bible tells us that when we are rejected, He too is rejected (Luke 10:16). We can begin to become free of rejection - we can see that Jesus was with us. We can begin to realise what He felt in that moment when we first experienced rejection. As we begin to see this, we can begin to believe that God has not abandoned us, and so we can start the journey of revelation to truly believe the verses that speak of the truth that He never leaves us.

You might be reading this and thinking it's easier said than done - you couldn't possibly understand. I agree, it is easier said than done. I have experienced feelings of rejection myself. I have felt unloved; I have felt as though I was on my own and that others were against me. Whilst I have some understanding of what you are feeling, I want to reassure you that Jesus understands:

'He was despised and rejected by mankind, a man of suffering, and familiar with pain. Like one from whom people hide their faces he was despised, and we held him in low esteem.'

Isaiah 53:3

We also read in the New Testament:

'About three in the afternoon Jesus cried out in a loud voice, "Eli, Eli, lama sabachthani?" (which means "My God, my God, why have you forsaken me?").'

Matthew 27:46

The verse in Isaiah (53:3) is foretelling Jesus' death where Jesus Himself will suffer rejection. We see in the verse in Matthew that Jesus asks Father why He has forsaken Him. We need to understand something here though. The love the Father has for Jesus is not being withdrawn. The Father is not rejecting Jesus nor turning away from Jesus. The Father is only turning away from our sin, which Jesus is taking upon Himself.

The Father is always close to His Son. The love the Father has for Jesus is the same love Jesus has for us (John 15:9). Therefore, just as the Father is always close to Jesus, so Jesus is close to us.

We also read:

'…Father, just as you are in me and I am in you. May they also be in us…'

John 17:21

Jesus is praying that we be in the Father in the same way that Jesus is in the Father and the Father is in Him. If we are in Jesus, then how is it possible for Him to not be with us? Again, we get picture of oneness. I think the Passion Translation provides a richer understanding of this verse:

'I pray for them all to be joined together as one even as you and I, Father, are joined together as one. I pray for them to become one with us…'

John 17:21 (TPT)

I encourage you, if you are feeling rejected, to allow this prayer of Jesus to penetrate your heart and the truth of those words to become louder than any feelings of rejection.

Part 2
Keys

Keys

We have looked at some of the prisons we might find ourselves in – now let's begin to look at ways in which we can begin to escape these prisons. Just like any prison door, there is a key which will unlock the door and enable us to walk into freedom.

The second part of the book is about leaving the prison and moving towards living in the palace - living in freedom as the Father wants us to. How do we move from one place to the other? What are the keys to breaking free from our prison? It's one thing to have the key in our hand, it can be another to use the key, especially when we have been locked up for so long. I am sure we've seen films where the main character is trapped or locked up, and then all of a sudden, they find a tool that will help them escape. Very often you can see hesitation; the character begins to question if this newly discovered tool is for real. I have good news! The keys we are going to discover together are for real! They are genuine ways in which we can begin to experience freedom.

The letter from James teaches us there is hope and that good things come from God:

'Every good and perfect gift is from above, coming down from the Father of the heavenly lights, who does not change like shifting sand.'

James 1:17

The keys come from our Father and they are available so that we might be free! Because they are from Him, the keys are good - they can be trusted. If we read this verse in The Passion translation, we discover the reason:

'so that we would fulfil his chosen destiny for us and become the favourite ones out of all creation.'

James 1:18b

The reason the keys are good and available for each of us to use, is to enable us to walk in our destiny and fulfil our purpose. Whilst we are locked up in these prisons, we have restricted freedom; we're unable to flourish and move into all that God has for us. We're inhibited from stepping into who He has created us to be. When we use the keys He provides, we can begin to walk free and into our true identity. When we are in the prisons, we can feel like we have no purpose. Satan wants to keep us feeling like we have no purpose - but God has a purpose for *every one of us* (Jeremiah 29:11). We need to use the keys that Father God has given us so that we live out the purpose that God has for each of us. It is important that we know what the keys are, and how we can use them.

How do we use the keys?

During an evening of worship, I was struggling with feelings of being back in a prison. As I lay on the floor surrendering all I was feeling and thinking to Him, I felt God say to me that He wanted to teach me to worship my way out of how I was feeling. He began to show me that one of my keys is worship. (We will look at this more in chapter 14). He showed me that even just lying there before the King and resting in His presence was worship. As we worship Him, everything we face and feel becomes nothing compared to who He is. What we are feeling and experiencing in the light of Jesus' majesty and glory pales into insignificance. We begin to see who He is, which is far greater and far superior than anything else. The writer to the Hebrews says:

'So he became as much superior to the angels as the name he has inherited is superior to theirs.'

Hebrews 1:4

Jesus is not just superior to the angels, but also to Moses (Hebrews 3:3-4), and Joshua (Hebrews 4:8-9). Jesus is a greater priest (Hebrews 7:26-28), a better covenant (Hebrews 7:22), and He is a better promise (Hebrews 8:6), and finally Jesus is a superior sacrifice (Hebrews 9:12). Hebrews teaches us that in every way, Jesus is superior and greater. There is nothing on earth that will not be subject to Him. He is above all. He is above every name (Philippians 2:9).

As we worship and come into His presence, He changes our perspective of what we came with, and we become wrapped into Him. Literally, His presence envelops everything else. He encouraged me to worship my way out and worship my way through the feelings and thoughts that were trying to imprison me again. I now had a different perspective. I want to be clear; this was not and is not a one-time thing. I didn't spend time lying in His presence and all of a sudden, the lies I was battling were gone. What it did was give me a route; a pathway for me to follow that directed me back to the palace.

If the keys I refer to represent a journey to help us out of the prison to the palace, we know a journey takes time and can take effort. When we start any journey, we don't find ourselves instantaneously at our destination. We travel the journey until we reach our destination. We may encounter roadblocks on our way, we may get diverted and find we need to use another road. There may be times we need to use another key, but we continue until we reach our destination. It is a process.

Whatever your key is, ask God how to use it. For each one of us there will be different uses, different things we should do, to get to our destination of the palace. Just like a journey, depending on where we are coming from will depend on how we get there. The destination is the same, the journey is different. My key will be different to yours, and yours will be different to someone else's.

I'm not convinced there is a 'master key'; one key for all eventualities. Just as there are different keys which unlock different doors, there are different keys for each of us to use, depending on the prison door we find ourselves at. In an earthly prison, a guard will have lots of different keys and each will unlock a different door. The guard knows which key unlocks which door. Therefore, we need to know which key to use on which door. There may be a time when you need to use a particular key, but that might lead to another door that requires a second key and so on. One thing we can be sure of is that as we use these keys to leave the prison we can then follow the path to our destination - the palace.

I want to encourage you there is a way out, and others can often help us on our journey. Have you ever been on a journey somewhere to discover you appear to be lost and you're not where you thought you were? Isn't it helpful to find someone who knows the area and can help to navigate you back onto the right path, or help you to on the next step on your journey? Maybe you've been in your local supermarket only to discover they have moved things around. The wisest and often the easiest thing is to ask someone who knows where the product you are looking for has been moved to.

The enemy will do all he can to confuse and distract you, and keep you from finding your way out of the prison. The devil wants you to feel like you're in solitary confinement; completely alone and the only one who can't get free. As with all things of the devil – it's a lie. You are not alone! Others want to be free of their prisons too and others have found freedom for themselves. Find someone who can help and encourage you on your journey.

We are more than conquerors and as such, freedom from every prison *is* possible if we walk the journey into freedom with Jesus.

I want to encourage you, as you read the second part of this book, to learn how the different keys work and continue to press in to find your way to freedom.

Promises

Each one of us has had promises made to us, and no doubt each of us has made promises to others. I'm sure in both cases we expect the promise to be kept. We understand what a promise is - when a promise is made, we expect that what is being promised will happen. One of my favourite television shows is 24 and the hero, Jack Bauer, often says "*You have my word.*" In essence, what he is saying is that he promises to do something. His word is his guarantee. For all the flaws of the hero, Jack's word is his word. He always fulfils what he says, no matter the cost to himself or others.

That's not true of all people. How many of us are still waiting on a promise from someone? How many of us have lost hope in that promise ever being fulfilled?

What about God? Have you ever received a promise from God? Do you have a certainty that He will fulfil what He says He will do? Most of us, I imagine, would respond '*yes*' to that question.

But honestly, when the rubber hits the road and things don't appear to be working out as you thought, can we always say '*yes*'? Would our '*yes*' be confident? Or would our '*yes*' become half-hearted? Maybe our response might be different to what we are believing in our hearts.

Perhaps you are reading this and thinking, but I don't have a promise from God. If this is the case, I encourage you to find promises in the bible that can help and encourage you. For example, if one of the prisons you feel locked in is rejection, you can hold on to the promise: *"I will never leave you nor forsake you."* (Deuteronomy 31:8).

I believe one of the keys to moving from the prison to the palace, is standing on His promises. I believe it is beneficial to remind ourselves of what He has spoken. One of the things I do, is keep a journal, a written log of the things God has spoken. You might already keep a journal of His words spoken to you, if so keep doing it, but also keep reading over them. If this is not your normal practice, I would encourage you to do so or find some other way to remind yourself of them. I believe His promises are a weapon to defeat the enemy. The enemy wants to stop us believing that God is faithful to His word. He uses tactics such as *"Did God really say?"* In those times when the circumstances around us are challenging; when the battle we are facing might seem impossible, the enemy will try to make us doubt God's promise over us. The devil wants to distract us from what God has promised and, thereby, cause us to instead look at the impossible situation. Maybe God spoke something to you such a long time ago that you've begun to lose hope in what He said, or maybe you've forgotten what He said? I believe we need to keep a hold of those promises and remind ourselves regularly of them. Don't lose sight of the promises He made to you. His promises help us be anchored to who He is - Faithful! Keeping hold of these promises enables us to continue to move forward towards the palace and not move back to living in the prison.

How can God's promises help us or encourage us?
When we are waiting for something to come to pass, the enemy can use this as an opportunity to cause us to question "*Did God really say…?*" During these times it is easy to question if God will come through this time.

Let's read some comforting verses from the Bible about the unchangeable nature of God's word.

When God makes a promise, He is making a covenant. He is saying that we *can* have complete trust and confidence that what He says will be fulfilled.

We read in Titus these comforting words:

'Paul, a servant of God and an apostle of Jesus Christ for the faith of God's elect and the knowledge of the truth that leads to godliness – a faith and knowledge resting on the hope of eternal life which ***God, who does not lie,*** *promised before the beginning of time…'*

Titus 1:1-2 (emphasis added)

God is not someone who can or will lie; He has never lied. What confidence we can have! Because of His nature, we can have hope in the certainty of His word to us.

We also read in Numbers:

'God is not a man, that he should lie, nor a son of man, that he should change his mind. Does he speak and then not act? Does he promise and not fulfil?'

Numbers 23:19

God is not like man whereby He could lie or change His mind. His word is binding. We also read here that the promises of God **are** fulfilled - if He speaks, He acts. In Hebrews, we read:

"When God made his promise to Abraham, since there was no one greater for him to swear by, he swore by himself…"

Hebrews 6:13

There is no greater authority than that of God Himself. Therefore, when He swears by Himself, He is providing assurance about what He is saying. Just like His unchanging character, so is His word. When He spoke it, He had all the relevant information needed to make that promise, therefore He will honour and fulfil it. So often, we might make a promise based on partial information, which subsequently means that we are unable to keep our promise. God is not like that. Many of us have heard someone say *'I swear on the Bible'* or something similar. In other words, this person is saying *'You can trust me'*; they are stating they are being completely honest. When God swears by Himself, we can have complete confidence in Him - we can completely trust what is being promised. His word is binding.

Let's take a look at Abraham and the promise that God made to him:

'The LORD had said to Abram, "Leave your country, your people and your father's household and go to the land I will show you. I will make you into a great nation and I will bless you; I will make your name great, and you will be a blessing."'

Genesis 12:1-2

At this point Abraham (known as Abram) didn't have any children; yet God promised to make him into a great nation. We read just a few chapters later in chapter 17:

'When Abram was ninety-nine years old, the LORD appeared to him and said: "I am God Almighty; walk before me and be blameless. I will confirm my covenant between me and you and will greatly increase your numbers." Abram fell face down, and God said to him, "As for me, this is my covenant with you: You will be the father of many nations, No longer will you be called Abram; your name will be Abraham, for I have made you a father of many nations. I will make you very fruitful; I will make nations of you, and kings will come from you."'

Genesis 17:1-6

What a promise! Notice that Abraham was an old man, he was ninety-nine years old. Yet despite his age, God was still going to fulfil His promise to him. God appears to go one step further; He confirms it to Abram in a sign. God changes Abram's name to Abraham, which means 'Father of many nations.' What a confirmation! As an old man, Abraham had his name changed to be an everlasting sign that God would fulfil His promise. I think it's important to remind ourselves here, that in the chapter before (chapter 16) Sarai (Sarah) had become tired of waiting on God. Sarai tells her husband to sleep with the maidservant (Genesis 16:2). It seems that Sarai was trying to solve the situation by herself; almost forcing God's promise to be outworked. At this point, it had been roughly 10 years since God's original promise to Abraham in chapter 12. How many of us after that length of time would have given up or tried to do it ourselves? Despite this, God doesn't forget His promise. We've seen that He reminds Abraham of His covenant and changes his name to help Abraham remember God's promise to him. (Genesis 17:5). This reminder comes some 23 years after God's original promise to Abraham. How often do we lose sight of a promise because it has not happened yet? How long have you been waiting? How much longer will you give God? Abraham received what was promised after waiting patiently (Hebrews 6:15). No matter how long we have been waiting God **will** fulfil his word.

Later, in the same chapter another conversation takes place between God and Abraham - this time about Sarah:

'God said to Abraham, "As for Sarai your wife, you are no longer to call her Sarai; her name will be Sarah. I will bless her and will surely give you a son by her. I will bless her so that she will be the mother of nations; kings of peoples will come from her." Abraham fell face down; he laughed and said to himself, "Will a son be born to a man a hundred years old? Will Sarah bear a child at the age of ninety?"... Then God said, "Yes, but your wife Sarah will bear you a son, and you will call him Isaac..."'

Genesis 17:15-17 and 19

In contrast to when Abraham fell face down (Genesis 17:3), this time he falls face down and laughs at what God says.[16] He has just received a covenantal sign of God's promise to him and has now been told that Sarah would be the mother of nations, even at the age of ninety. Abraham appears to be able to believe God for himself, but not for a woman of that age. Notice God's response - "*Yes*". I can almost hear the loving laughter in God's voice. The irony in this of course is that the name Isaac means 'God is laughing.' There is a sense of God saying "*Of course, I can do anything.*"

You may be familiar with the rest of the story. God *does* fulfil His promise to Abraham. Some passages in the New Testament about Abraham's story encourage us further; they can reassure us in our time of waiting and cause our faith and hope to grow.

Let's start with Hebrews 11, that great chapter of faith:

'By faith Abraham, even though he was past age – and Sarah herself was barren – was enabled to become a father because **he considered him faithful who had made the promise**. *And so from this one man, and* **he was as good as dead**, *came descendants as numerous as the stars in the sky and countless as the sand on the seashore.'*

Hebrews 11:11-12 (emphasis added)

Abraham was as good as dead. He was an old man who was beyond child-bearing age, as was Sarah, who was barren. In the natural, this couple had no hope of walking into the promise that

16 Also in Genesis 18 we read of a time when Sarah laughs at God, after being told that in 1 year she would have a son.

God had made to them. You can understand why Sarah tried to take matters into her own hands. What other chance was there? Yet, despite all that, although Abraham laughed at God (Genesis 17:17) we also read in the verse in Hebrews that Abraham considered God to be faithful to the promise He made. Despite the circumstances or situations we face, we too can have the same hope. Have you been waiting a long time for something God promised you? Does it feel like He has forgotten you or the promise? Do you sometimes feel like giving up hope, or maybe trying to do it yourself? Do you find yourself feeling like you're back in that prison? I want to encourage you no matter where you are on your journey to freedom that God **is** faithful. He is not a liar.

Jesus is the reason we can have confidence in God.

'"or no matter how many promises God has made, they are "Yes" in Christ. And so through him the "Amen" is spoken by us to the glory of God.'

2 Corinthians 1:20

All of God's promises, no matter how many there are, are yes in Christ. We can simply put our Amen[17] to them. We can and should come into agreement with the promises He has made.

Let's look at one more passage regarding the promise to Abraham. This is what Paul writes in his letter to the Romans about Abraham:

[17] Amen means: So be it.

*'**Against all hope,** Abraham in hope believed and so became the father of many nations, just as it had been said to him. "So shall your offspring be." Without weakening in his faith, he faced the fact that his body was as good as dead – since he was about one hundred years old – and that Sarah's womb was also dead. Yet he **did not waver** in unbelief regarding the promise of God, but was **strengthened in his faith** and gave glory to God, being **fully persuaded that God had power to do what he promised.**'*

Romans 4:18-21 (emphasis added)

According to Paul, there was no hope humanly speaking of the promise being fulfilled. However, Paul goes on to say that Abraham had hope and did not waver. Once Abraham believed, his faith didn't weaken. Something inside Abraham gave him the strength to believe. He had a confidence, and it appears the answer to his unwavering, was his faith in God. It was this that gave him peace. No matter what others may have said to him; no matter what Sarah said - Abraham was persuaded that God would do what He said He would do. He had gone on a journey of understanding the faithfulness of God's promises. Therefore, for Abraham it was now as simple as He said it, therefore He will do it.

Let's use the story of Abraham to encourage us! If God did it once, if God broke all human boundaries to fulfil a promise, then surely He can do it for you too. For Abraham, nothing was impossible for God (Luke 1:37).

As Peter says, God is never late on delivering His promises:

'The Lord is not slow in keeping his promise.'

1 Peter 3:9

I once heard Bill Johnson say in a talk "*No freshly spoken word of God will ever come to you that does not contain its own ability to perform itself.*"

This well-known verse in Isaiah also reminds us of the power in God's words to accomplish what He intends them to:

'so is my word that goes out from my mouth: It will not return to me empty, but will accomplish what I desire and achieve the purpose for which I sent it.'

Isaiah 55:11

Throughout this chapter we've seen no matter what the circumstances around us might be or situations we face - God is a God who *always* keeps His word! He can turn the impossibilities of our circumstances, and any lies we believe, into hope and life. He can and does free us from the prisons we feel locked in. As I have previously said I encourage you to write down the promises He has given you; the ones you feel have not yet come to pass. As you write those promises down, remind yourself of them. Begin to see your situations through the lens of His promises. Allow the promises to burn brighter, with the truth of who He is. What are the situations you face? What are the lies you are still believing? Allow the promises of God to speak hope and let them be the weapon to defeat the enemy. The enemy has no response to God's promises. What are the promises He has spoken to you? What are the promises in His word about those situations you face? Allow these promises to be a key to your breakthrough, because as Paul says in Thessalonians:

'The one who calls you is faithful, and he will do it.'

1 Thessalonians 5:24

Forgiveness

Forgiveness is often an easy concept to understand, but it can be challenging to actually put into practice at times. Very often we know we *should* forgive the one who has offended or hurt us, but when it comes to actually forgiving, we can often have second thoughts. The hurt may feel too big. Have you ever encouraged a friend to forgive someone, but realised you haven't followed your own advice? Perhaps someone has hurt us so profoundly that we found ourselves thinking or saying something like: "*I will never forgive them for that.*" We have, in that moment, made a vow - a commitment or a promise to not forgive.

You may be thinking "*You don't understand what that person did. If they had done to you what they did to me, then you would understand. If I forgive this person, it will feel like they've got away with it.*". We might feel the person should be punished for what they did. Maybe we think they don't deserve our forgiveness.

I don't know what people have done to hurt you and I may not fully understand all you have been though. However, I've ministered to many people who have experienced a range of painful experiences and, as they began to forgive, they found this started the process of releasing the hurt they had been holding on to. They had been the ones hurting and not the person who hurt them. Forgiveness is often a process, as is the healing from the hurt caused.

A doctor at the Harvard Medical School identified that when somebody chooses to not forgive, they become trapped by the actions of those who hurt them. The person choosing unforgiveness focuses on the actions of those that hurt them and consequently they experience negative thoughts and anger.[18] Unforgiveness holds us captive.

Let's look at the example Jesus provides us, in relation to forgiveness. Just before Jesus was hung on the cross, He said:

'Father if you are willing, take this cup from me; yet not my will, but yours be done.'

Luke 22:42

---

[18] https://www.health.harvard.edu/mind-and-mood/the-power-of-forgiveness (accessed October 2023)

Jesus here is praying to His Father that there might be another way. Jesus knew the agony, pain and torture He was about to experience.

In the next chapter when Jesus is on the cross:

Jesus said, "Father, forgive them, for they do not know what they are doing.'"

Luke 23:34

Jesus spoke these words having been beaten, humiliated, ridiculed, tortured and much more. He was close to a painful death, and yet He still chose to forgive His aggressors.

It's worth reminding ourselves that Jesus hung there as a man, not as God:

'Who, being in very nature God, did not consider equality with God something to be grasped, but made himself nothing, taking the very nature of a servant, being made in human likeness. And being found in appearance as a man, he humbled himself and became obedient to death – even death on a cross!'

Philippians 2:6-8

Paul is teaching us that whilst on earth, Jesus was fully man. He was humiliated and tortured and yet He chose to forgive.

I highlight the example of Jesus to encourage us that even in the most horrendous suffering we can still choose forgiveness. Jesus understood the importance of forgiveness and He modelled to us true forgiveness. He was encouraging us that we too can forgive.

I believe that forgiveness is a choice. We can either choose to forgive or not. There is no middle ground. Often, however, forgiveness is a process, a process that we *must* begin. We may not feel like it right now, but as we forgive, our feelings and emotions will catch up. Therefore, as we continue to forgive, it will become easier. I want to encourage you to begin the process of forgiving today; maybe begin to say out loud *"I choose forgive (insert name)…."* A moving ship is easier to steer than one that is stationary. In other words, as you begin to forgive, and you say the words *"I choose to forgive…"* you start to move forward, and so it will become easier to continue to forgive.

A while ago I was praying with a lady and I felt Father say to me *"She needs to forgive."* I didn't know who she needed to forgive or what for, I simply felt the prompting of Father. I shared with this person, and to be honest she didn't respond. I left it with her, and I didn't enquire any further in that moment. I trusted that if that was Father, then He would do what He needed to do. About two months later this same lady came up to me and explained that at first she didn't feel the word was right for her; she couldn't think of anyone she needed to forgive. She went on to explain that a few days after I shared the word she began to cry for no apparent reason. She went on to explain that as she cried, she asked God why she was crying and He said *"It's because of your mum, you need to forgive her"*. My word about forgiveness started the process of this lady recognising that forgiveness was needed. This lady explained that over the next few weeks, as she continued to forgive her mum, the issue I had been originally praying for was answered. She got healed. Sometimes (but not always), there can be a link between unforgiveness and physical pain.[19] Let me encourage you with another testimony. My wife and I led a lady through a process of forgiving. The following morning the lady got in touch to tell us that longstanding sores in her mouth had disappeared; she believed it was a direct link to her choosing to forgive.

Forgiveness can be one of the most challenging things we can choose to do. However, I believe forgiveness is also one of the best things we can do. The rewards are far greater.

The following saying is well known; *"Unforgiveness is drinking poison yourself and waiting for the other person to die."*[20] In other words, when we don't forgive, we are the ones who get hurt, not the offender.

Sometimes we can misunderstand what forgiveness means. This could be due to not fully recognising the effect unforgiveness can have upon us. Therefore, let's spend a moment looking at what forgiveness is not, then with that understanding we get a clearer picture of what forgiveness is.

What forgiveness is not

Sometimes we feel we can't forgive somebody because we cannot forget what they did. We might think that forgiving means forgetting. Just because we choose to forgive doesn't mean we forget what happened. Let's be honest, that can often be impossible. Forgiving does not mean forgetting. However, as

---

[19] https://www.hopkinsmedicine.org/health/wellness-and-prevention/forgiveness-your-health-depends-on-it (accessed May 2024)
[20] Marianne Williamson Quotes. (n.d.). BrainyQuote.com. Retrieved May 10, 2024, from BrainyQuote.com Web site: https://www.brainyquote.com/quotes/marianne_williamson_635346

we forgive it enables the process to start, thereby allowing Father to remove the emotional pain and hurt associated with what happened. Therefore, if and when we remember what occurred, the associated pain and hurt reduce. Just like an insect bite can often be itchy, when we put a cream on it the bite mark is still there, but the itchiness no longer has an effect. Forgiveness takes the sting out of the bite.

Forgiveness doesn't mean we *have* to be reconciled with the one who hurt us. When someone hurts us, at times it can be so serious that they have lost our trust. Trust is something that has to be earned. When I was a teenager, I confided in a friend something I didn't want anyone else to know. I thought I could trust him. However, he then told others. Although I forgave him, I chose not to continue to confide in him. It is important to keep healthy boundaries, but I want to encourage you that forgiveness can be a significant step towards reconciliation, but this will often depend on the specific situation.

Forgiveness doesn't mean that the offending person has the freedom to repeat their actions. If we forgive, we are not permitting the wrong we have suffered to be repeated. When Jesus teaches us to "turn the other cheek" (Luke 6:29) He is not saying we are allowing that person to do it again, nor is He saying that we should be happy for that thing to have happened. What Jesus is teaching us is the true meaning of forgiveness.

I've heard people say if I forgive the person who hurt me, that will somehow justify what the person did. Forgiveness doesn't defend or excuse the action of that person. Forgiveness is about releasing the person that hurt us from any judgement we may have made about them. Only God can judge people's attitudes and hearts.

What forgiveness is

So having looked at what forgiveness is not, let's begin to look at what forgiveness *is*.

The passage in Luke 6:29 (mentioned above) teaches us the true meaning of forgiveness. This involves entrusting the offending person to God. Jesus is teaching us that even when we have been hurt or wronged, no matter how severely, we don't have the right to retaliate or seek revenge. Forgiveness is giving up our right to retaliate.

Forgiveness is choosing to hand the person who has wronged us to God and into His care and responsibility, even if it means that person seemingly never answers for what they have done.[21] It is about stepping down from the judgment seat and leaving it in the hands of The Judge - Jesus. The One who is the perfect judge. Forgiveness is saying I trust God to deal with that person how He pleases. It's a change of heart.

If unforgiveness locks us in a prison, choosing to forgive is saying I want to free myself up to be healed of that wrong done to me and move forward. It's saying I no longer want to be locked up in the prison of unforgiveness.

Let's have a look at the parable of the Unmerciful Servant to see the effect that unforgiveness can have upon us:

---

[21] I am not saying that serious wrongs such as murder, rape etc. should not go unpunished. The punishment is not ours to carry out.

'Therefore, the kingdom of heaven is like a king who wanted to settle accounts with his servants. As he began the settlement, a man who owed him ten thousand bags of gold was brought to him. Since he was not able to pay, the master ordered that he and his wife and his children and all that he had be sold to repay the debt. "The servant fell on his knees before him. 'Be patient with me,' he begged, 'and I will pay back everything.' The servant's master took pity on him, cancelled the debt and let him go. "But when that servant went out, he found one of his fellow servants who owed him a hundred silver coins. He grabbed him and began to choke him. 'Pay back what you owe me!' he demanded. "His fellow servant fell to his knees and begged him, 'Be patient with me, and I will pay it back.' "But he refused. Instead, he went off and had the man thrown into prison until he could pay the debt. When the other servants saw what had happened, they were outraged and went and told their master everything that had happened. "Then the master called the servant in. 'You wicked servant,' he said, 'I cancelled all that debt of yours because you begged me to. Shouldn't you have had mercy on your fellow servant just as I had on you?' In anger his master handed him over to the jailers to be tortured, until he should pay back all he owed. "This is how my heavenly Father will treat each of you unless you forgive your brother or sister from your heart."'

Matthew 18:23-35

The king had forgiven a large debt owed to him by the servant; instead of having to pay it back, the servant and his family were able to go free. However, the forgiven servant was not willing to forgive the one who had a debt toward him. He had not learned the power of forgiveness. He hadn't recognised the freedom he now enjoyed because he had been forgiven, and as a result of his unforgiveness, the master put him back into prison until he paid back all he owed. The servant couldn't pay it back. All the servant needed to have done was choose to forgive the debt that was owed to him, to stay out of prison. The master says in verse 33: *"Shouldn't you have mercy of your fellow servant."* Mercy was the only way out of his prison. The only way for the forgiven servant to be free was for he, himself, to extend that same forgiveness.

Jesus is quite clear in Matthew:

'For if you forgive men when they sin against you, your Heavenly Father will also forgive you, but if you do not forgive men their sins, your Father will not forgive your sins.'

Matthew 6:14-15

Our forgiving of others is based on our revelation of how much we are forgiven. We are compelled to forgive because we are forgiven.

Jesus is commanding us to forgive, but He gives us the freedom to choose to forgive. Jesus knows the importance for us to forgive, therefore His command to forgive comes out of His love for us. He doesn't want us to carry the effects of unforgiveness.

In the passage above from Matthew 6 Jesus appears to be speaking to his disciples; because it says in Matthew 5:1 that Jesus moved away from the crowds to a mountain and His disciples came to Him. He is therefore speaking to believers. Jesus is *not* saying here that if you don't forgive then you will not receive His forgiveness that leads to salvation. Those listening to Him here have already received that. The forgiveness of sin we receive at the point of salvation is not in question here. The Bible is very clear that if we confess our sins, He will forgive us (1 John 1:9).

Jesus' teaching in Matthew 6 refers to the forgiveness that is necessary in our continued fellowship with Father God. If I argue with my wife, until we forgive each other there will be a distance between us. Will we continue to love each other? Yes. Will we still talk? Of course. But until forgiveness takes place, we don't have the same intimacy with each other. In the same way, there is a barrier between us and Father God when we hold on to unforgiveness.

We have received forgiveness freely from Him, how much more then should we forgive others? We received forgiveness that we didn't deserve, it was unmerited. Jesus chose to die that we might receive grace from our Father in Heaven and be completely forgiven! When we truly understand this, we become more willing to forgive those who have wronged us.

I said at the beginning of this chapter that forgiveness is a choice, but it is also a command. We are told to forgive because God forgave us.

'Bear with each other and forgive whatever grievances you may have against one another. Forgive as the Lord forgave you.'

Colossians 3:13.

Paul also encourages us in Ephesians to:

'Be kind and compassionate to one another, forgiving each other, just as in Christ God forgave you.'

Ephesians 4:32

It is with the backdrop of the forgiveness we have received from Father that we are encouraged to forgive one another.

The love the Father has for us, outweighs what has been done to us. It's that same love and forgiveness that compels us to forgive others. God is a loving Father and He knows how important it is that we forgive one another. If we find ourselves holding on to pain, bitterness, and anger; these feelings could ultimately hurt us more than the original wrongdoing. Father does not want us to carry painful emotions. It's in the action of forgiving others, that we begin to let go of any pain, bitterness, or anger we may be holding onto and as we give that to Jesus, He then can set us free.

Unforgiveness keeps us in the prison which we have been trying to escape from. As we forgive, we begin to see this is the key to unlocking the prison door; and our journey to the palace can begin.

I want to encourage you to begin the process of forgiving anyone who has done wrong to you. No matter how hard it is, remember that you do not have to say it to them personally. They may not even realise they have hurt you. Forgiveness is between you and Father God. Say to God "*Today I choose to forgive…for…*" Then give any negative emotions, for example betrayal, to Jesus and ask Him to begin to release your heart from the hurt that has been caused. Ask Him what He wants to give you in exchange for the hurt you have let go of.[22] Allow Him to show you how much He loves you, and what He thinks about you. You most likely won't forget what happened to you, but the pain and hurt

[22] Based on a Bethel Sozo tool

will begin to subside. You may need to do the same tomorrow and the next day and so on. However, over time you will realise that even when you remember the situation that originally hurt you, the pain is no longer there, or you may be able to think about that person without thinking of the hurt that was caused.

I encourage you to continue on this journey of forgiveness. Remember - forgiveness is for your sake and your good. Forgiveness begins to remove any barrier there may be between you and Father that was caused by holding on to unforgiveness. Forgiveness is a powerful and significant key to leaving behind our prisons and walking into the Palace.

"To forgive is to set a prisoner free and discover that the prisoner was you."[23]

---

[23] Lewis B Smedes. (n.d.). BrainyQuote.com. Retrieved June 2024, from BrainyQuote.com Web site: https://www.brainyquote.com/lists/authors/top-10-lewis-b-smedes-quotes

Renew our Minds

Renewing our mind; thinking about ourselves the way God does and thinking rightly about who He is, is important. I firmly believe renewing our minds is a crucial key to use as we move from the prison to the palace. When our thinking becomes more in line with God's, it becomes easier to journey to the palace.

Let's look at what the Bible says about renewing our mind:

'Do not ***conform*** *to the pattern of this world, but be* ***transformed*** *by the* ***renewing*** *of your mind...'*

Romans 12:2 (emphasis added)

Or as the Message version puts it:

'Don't become so well adjusted to your culture that you fit into it even without thinking. Instead, fix your attention on God. You'll be changed

from the inside out.'

Romans 12:2 (Msg)

Conform

So often our culture and those around us affect the way we think. We might listen to the news or read something that influences our thoughts or behaviour. Paul says that we must *not* conform to the world around us. Elsewhere, Jesus says that we are not of this world (John 17:14-17). If we live in the world, how can it not affect the way we think? Simply put; we need to think differently.

When someone conforms, they do as others do. They see something or hear something and imitate that behaviour. Conformity means to imitate or copy. The Passion Translation puts it this way:

'Stop imitating the ideals and opinions of the culture around you…'

Romans 12:2a (TPT)

We are being encouraged to stop thinking as the world thinks. We have the mind of Christ (1 Corinthians 2:16); we should conform to a Kingdom mentality. We can think how Jesus thinks. We don't have to be swayed by the world around us - we *can* think differently. Instead of being influenced, we can be the ones who positively influence how others think. I have a friend who thinks differently to me. I'm not by nature a negative person, but my friend always thinks bigger than I do. His outlook is one of faith and when he speaks, he imparts faith. I am constantly challenged by him in a good way! He positively affects my thinking. I encourage you to listen to those around you who challenge you to think more like Christ. When we have a renewed mind, we begin to think and speak more like Jesus.

Transformed

Instead of conforming to the world, we can be transformed! When someone is transformed, they are changed. The Greek word *'metamorphoo'* used in Romans 12:2 is the same word used in the transfiguration in Matthew 17:2. The message here therefore is that we can completely change into another form.[24]

We are being encouraged to change the way we think. The New Living Translation says:

'Don't copy the behaviour and customs of this world, but let God transform you into a new person by changing the way you think'

Romans 12:2 (NLT)

As we change the way we think, we see that we are transformed into a new person. Bill Johnson says:

"It's not that our thoughts are different, but that our way of thinking is transformed because we think from a different reality." [25]

We can think from the perspective of Heaven and not the perspective of the world. As we do this, we become transformed.

---

[24] https://www.blueletterbible.org/lexicon/g3339/kjv/tr/0-1/ (accessed January 2023)
[25] Johnson, B. (2005), *The Supernatural Power of a Transformed Mind*. Destiny Image. P.42. (Permission granted)

I quoted the first part of this same verse in The Passion Translation earlier, let's now look at the next part:

'...be inwardly transformed by the Holy Spirit through a total reformation of how you think.'

Romans 12:2b (TPT)

It's through the power of the Holy Spirit that we can think differently. It is the Holy Spirit who dwells within us that enables us to think from the reality of Heaven.

Renew

We've seen that we're not to think like the world, but instead, think from a heavenly perspective. So how do we do that?

Paul says by renewing our minds (Romans 12:2). Our spiritual transformation starts in our minds. As He lives within us, we can think like Christ. We are to adjust our focus. Rather than being influenced by the world around us, as we focus on the truth of the Kingdom of Heaven, we then become influenced by its values and culture. We can have a new attitude, the attitude of Heaven. As Bill Johnson says:

"The renewed mind, then reflects the reality of another world" [26]

As we focus on Heaven and think the way Jesus thinks, we begin to be transformed. It is more than not conforming to the world around us, instead we can have an influence on it. Paul is saying

---

[26] Johnson, B. (2005), *The Supernatural Power of a Transformed Mind.* Destiny Image. P.42. (Permission granted)

that as we begin to think the way Heaven thinks about us, then you will become changed. I once heard the phrase "*Be a thermostat and not a thermometer.*" In other words, we are to set the culture, we are to be the influencer.

How?

How can we begin to renew our minds? The best place to start is the bible. What does the bible say about the nature of God? What does the bible say about who we are? We need to immerse ourselves in His truth, His thoughts. Maybe you have some memory verses you can declare over yourself. In Luke 4 Jesus used scripture to overcome the temptation of the devil. As we read, mediate on, and declare scripture, we will overcome the lies of the enemy.

I've compiled a short list of some of the truths about our identity from scripture, to help us overcome the lies of the enemy. You will find these in the Appendix.

Is there a lie you are believing about yourself or about the nature of God? Ask God to show you where you first believed that lie. Maybe someone spoke it over you or did something that caused you to believe the lie. If so, choose to forgive that person, come out of agreement with the lie and ask God to show you what His truth is.[27]

Purpose

What is the purpose of renewing our mind? What is the outcome of having a renewed mind and thinking from the reality of Heaven? Paul continues by saying:

---

[27] This process was described in more detail in chapter 3; 'Lies'.

'Then you will be able to test and approve what God's will is – his good, pleasing and perfect will.'

Romans 12:2

Or as the Message version puts it:

'Readily recognise what he wants from you, and quickly respond to it…'

Romans 12:2 (Msg)

With a renewed mind we can identify God's truths from the enemy's lies. We can know His heart; we can know His thoughts. There is no more confusion. We can have clarity and an understanding of who He is and who He says we are. Bill Johnson puts it this way:

"I can't afford to have a thought in my head about me that He does not have in His head about me".[28]

Renewing our minds helps us to think about ourselves the way He thinks about us. A renewed mind is like a protective shield because, whilst we may hear the lie of the enemy, we already know the truth of Heaven.

Paul in 2nd Corinthians says:

'We demolish arguments and every pretension that sets itself up against the knowledge of God, and we take captive every thought to make it

---

[28] Johnson, B. (2016), *God is Good: He's Better than you Think.* Destiny Image P45. (Permission granted)

obedient to Christ.'

2 Corinthians 10:5

When thoughts come to us that don't align with Heaven - we can take them captive and not allow them to influence our mind. We can ask ourselves '*does this thought line up with the nature of God and His promises for me?*' If the answer is no, then we have the power through the Holy Spirit, to reject the lie and its effect on us. We can then declare the truth of God and His word.

Renewing our mind also encompasses identifying any negative thought patterns that may have developed over time. Examples of this could be thinking we're worthless, we'll never amount to anything, or that we're stupid.

How we think about ourselves usually originates from when we were young children. Perhaps a parent or teacher said something negative about us; and at that young age we don't have the capacity to filter lies from truth. Therefore, the more we hear these negative words spoken about us the more they become ingrained and over time we begin to believe the negative statement is true. We begin to agree with the lie and eventually this can become our way of thinking. We begin to see our life through that lens, for example - through the lens of worthlessness. However, with a renewed mind we can make daily choices to think like Christ, we can choose to think from the perspective of Heaven. Does Heaven think I am worthless? Does that line up with the word of God? We read passages that say we are fearfully and wonderfully made (Psalm 139:14), and that He chose us before the creation of the world (Ephesians 1:4). Do these truths agree with the thought of being worthless?

No!

Our behaviour can be influenced by the way we think. Let's look at a verse from Proverbs:

'For as he thinks in his heart, so is he.'

Proverbs 23:7 (NKJV)

What we think about ourselves ultimately affects who we are. If we have negative thoughts or allow the lies of the enemy to influence us, we will not see ourselves as God sees us. Paul encourages us in Ephesians to have a different attitude and to have the attitude of Heaven:

'be made new in the attitude of our minds.'

Ephesians 4:23

I encourage you to regularly spend time renewing your mind. We should be aware of our thoughts, and ensuring they line up with God's truth. As we do that, we are made new. The process of being transformed is continuous. It is something which *has* already happened as we have been transformed by the regenerative power of the Holy Spirit; but we can also continually be transformed. It is a process I encourage you to embrace.

If we don't actively pursue a renewed mind, we will struggle as we listen to lies from the enemy. We will find it more difficult to live from the palace perspective.

Let's read that same verse in The Passion Translation:

'Now it's time to be made new by every revelation that's been given to you. And to be transformed as you embrace the glorious Christ within as your new life and live in union with him!'

Ephesians 4:23-24a (TPT)

What a thought! As we embrace the truth that Christ lives within us, and receive the revelation of who He is, and who He made us to be, then we are transformed! Notice that the time is 'now.' There is never a better time to start the journey of renewing our minds than now.

There have been many times as I have been ministering to people where God shows them they are believing a lie. I remember one such time when ministering to a gentleman. He felt God show him he was believing the lie that God would hurt the few to save the many. It was like a lightbulb lit up in his mind. He realised he believed this lie because of how his earthly father had behaved. He said, *"God isn't like that is He?"* There are many lies we believe simply because of what people have said to us or how they have behaved.

We need to allow His word to renew our minds and change our belief system, so that we can be transformed into the person He wants us to be. So often the false things we believe about ourselves are the very things that hold us back and will keep us in the prison we long to escape from. I'm still surprised by the subtle lies that God shows me I am believing. I have to continually speak the truth of His word over my life.

It is important, as we go through the process of renewing our minds, that we speak out the truths. Jesus says in Luke:

'For out of the overflow of his heart his mouth speaks.'

Luke 6:45b

Therefore, let's declare out loud the truth of who God says we are, let's allow our minds to be renewed and start believing it as truth.

Let us start to speak life into our minds. Remember:

'The tongue has the power of life and death …'

Proverbs 18:21

Fruit of a renewed mind

What would your life look like with a renewed mind? For me, I have been able to more easily live from the perspective of Heaven. I have begun to believe the things the Bible says God thinks about me.

As our minds are renewed, we can see life the way God sees life. We no longer allow the negative experiences or challenges in life, or the prison we face, to influence our thinking but allow God's truths to shape our thought patterns.

When we have a renewed mind, we begin to see God for who He truly is. We begin to believe God is bigger than the circumstances, we can say with more certainty that God is good. We begin to realise that with God all things are possible

(Matthew 19:26). We can depend on Him, fully!

When we have a renewed mind, we can silence the lie of the enemy. The renewed mind recognises a lie and can declare that is not true because God says this about me. The truth of God's thoughts towards us are louder than the lies of the enemy.

I want to encourage you to continue the process of renewing your minds and begin to move from the prison to the palace. With a renewed mind, it is easier to overcome that which seem to hold us back.

No matter what the old thought patterns you had are, God wants to give you a new focus, a fresh hope and a new reality. It is time to believe the hope and freedom that God provides. It is time to change our thinking and be transformed so we truly believe how *He* sees us and feels about us. Let's pursue renewing our mind to walk out of the prison we're in and walk towards our home, the palace.

Perspective

Have you noticed how different people can view something in a completely different way than you do? For example, at a football match if you speak with a supporter of the home team, no matter how well their team played or not, they will have a different take on the match to the away side. Yet someone with an impartial view might reflect on the match differently again.

I remember when I was at Bible college, the entire class (about 50 of us) were asked to look out the same window for about 5 minutes at the same time, and then write down the things we noticed during that time. It was interesting to note that whilst many of us observed certain things the same way, it was also true that we also observed things differently. It was like we were looking through 50 different windows. The purpose of the exercise was to show us how the four Gospels, although with some similarities had many differences, and yet were still accurate. Each of the four Gospel writers had a different upbringing and background. They had a different way of looking at life, and consequently they viewed and reported the life of Jesus in a way that was shaped by who they were and their unique perspective of life.

It is also true of our individual giftings, whether that be a spiritual gift or a natural gift.

Take, for example each of the leadership gifts in Ephesians 4, often described as the five-fold ministries:

'It was he who gave some to be apostles, some to be prophets, some to be evangelists, and some to be pastors and teachers.'

Ephesians 4:11

Leaders with these giftings will view situations and life through the lens of their particular gifting.

Our life experiences, personalities and giftings (amongst other things) influence how we view life.

Paul writes in his first letter to the church in Corinth:

'For now we are looking in a mirror that gives only a dim (blurred) reflection [of reality], but then we shall see in reality and face to face!'

1 Corinthians 13:12 (AMP)

Whilst living here on earth we are going to see things differently from the perspective of Heaven. However, Paul doesn't stop there, he continues by saying when we are in Heaven *then* we shall see clearly. Our earthly perspective is not the perspective that God wants us to view life from. He has a better perspective; He has a better view - a clearer view.

Lenses

I wear glasses and I remember a time when I had to change my glasses. I had a new prescription, and as I put these new glasses on it felt like I was seeing in high definition. I hadn't realised how distorted my vision was when looking through a pair of glasses that were no longer suitable for my eyes. When these old pair of glasses were new, my vision was clear. Over time that clarity changed, and without me recognising it, I was no longer seeing with the same precision or clarity.

Sometimes it can be the same with how we view life. We've become so accustomed with seeing things in a certain way, that our understanding of who God is may also become distorted. For example, if we continually see life through the lens of rejection, we might begin to feel like God has also rejected us.

You may know the phrase "*looking through rose-tinted glasses*"? It means seeing life in such a way that everything is always fine and rosy. We only see the good and positive in the circumstances we face. For example, in the autumn the trees begin to change colour and eventually the leaves begin to fall off. We see this is allowing room for new growth. However, if we look through lenses that distort the picture, we could see this same natural event as the tree dying. We see it from a negative viewpoint. I remember someone commenting on something I had done. They were being positive and encouraging, but I didn't hear it that way. I had become so used to thinking people didn't encourage me, that even when these encouraging words were spoken to me, I heard them as a discouragement. I had become so accustomed to thinking a certain way that even a compliment was turned around to be a criticism. I was interpreting life through a negative lens.

When we face challenging circumstances, the enemy might begin to whisper his lies to us that can begin to alter our perspective, but this will not be the perspective of Heaven. The enemy wants us to feel hopeless and defeated.

My wife and I had the privilege of ministering to a lady who explained over many years she had been told she wouldn't amount to anything and that she was useless. As such, she saw anything she did as worthless and having no value. As she gave these false lenses[29] of unworthiness to God, she asked Him what lenses He wanted to give her in return. She was given lenses of truth. God said to her, "*I am the truth, you can now see through my eyes.*" This lady now had a new perspective. She had new lenses, and she could see things as Jesus saw them.

When we begin to look from Heaven's perspective, we can begin to see with a clearer view.

Let's look at the final words of Jesus on the cross:

'It is finished'

John 19:30

---

[29] Based on a Bethel Sozo tool.

These final words from Jesus were heard by different groups of people with different perspectives and, as we shall see, the words had different meanings to each group.

The first group were the Romans. The Roman's perspective of Jesus was as a troublesome revolutionary. To them these final words of Jesus were words of His defeat; it was a cry that said it was all over. The Romans heard this and had cause to celebrate, a revolutionary had been killed off. He was one less problem to worry about. This was a cry of success for the Romans.

The second group that heard this cry were the Jewish leaders. To this group these words represented the end of the Jesus movement. Jesus had challenged their temple practices (Matthew 21:12) and their authority. So, when Jesus cried these words, the Jewish leaders heard Jesus saying, "*You win*". They heard the words as defeat for the Jesus movement and success for them; the biggest threat to their belief system was now dead.

The third group of people who heard the cry of Jesus were those people who had put their hope in Him; the ones who had spent 3 years following Him. The disciples. It was these people who would have been hit the hardest. The disciples had seen His miracles, they watched and listened as He proclaimed the good news. The disciples hoped their teacher, their leader, was the One. When Jesus cried these words, their hope turned to fear. Their leader, their Messiah had been killed, and they feared they would be next. The disciples heard the words "*it is finished*" and to them it would have meant "*we are finished.*" To the disciples, this was a cry of pain and loss. It was a cry that meant confusion. Now what were they to do?

Three groups of people with different perspectives, three different interpretations of the words *"it is finished"*. But there is one more perspective we haven't yet looked at. It is this perspective that is the most astounding. It is the view of Jesus Himself, the perspective of Heaven. It's the perspective He wants us to look from.

To Jesus these three words *'It is finished'* are *not* a cry of defeat or death or despair. Jesus is *not* saying, "*I give up, you win*", He is *not* saying, "*I lost, it's all over.*" No - quite the opposite! There is no defeat in these words from the perspective of Jesus. These words from the perspective of Heaven are a cry of victory! The words are a cry of hope. The words are a cry of declaration. The words "*It is finished*" are a call to celebrate!

At the moment of the Cross when Jesus spoke out *'It is finished'* the disciples didn't want to celebrate. However, had they heard the words from Jesus's perspective, they could now celebrate, they had the victory. Jesus was all they believed Him to be. When the Romans and the Jewish leaders heard the words and thought they could celebrate as victors, from the perspective of Jesus suddenly their plans were defeated, they had no cause to celebrate. Their party was over. From Heaven's perspective these words have a completely different meaning, the mood changes. Where there was once no hope, there is now hope. Where there were once tears, there is now joy. These words of Jesus are the most powerful words ever spoken. They changed the course of history. *"It is finished"* meant it is accomplished, everything that needed to be done was fulfilled on the Cross. They are words that provided hope and a future to a group that thought they had lost it all. They are words that still today provide hope and a future, they are words that today still have as much power in them as when they were first spoken. They are words that today continue to ring in the ears of satan and fill him with fear and dread. You see - the situations that you face, the struggles the enemy wants to imprison you with, are the very things that Jesus says, "*It is finished*" over. You can have hope; you do have the victory!

It's time to look at the circumstances we face through the lens of the Cross. We can see the situations in our life through Jesus' cry of victory: "*It is finished.*"

How do we change our perspective? I will look more closely at this in Part 3, but for now let's look at another story with two perspectives; the story of Joshua and Caleb exploring Canaan:

'When Moses sent them to explore Canaan, he said, "Go up through the Negev and on into the hill country. See what the land is like and whether the people who live there are strong or weak, few or many. What kind of land do they live in? Is it good or bad? What kind of towns do they live in? Are they unwalled or fortified? How is the soil? Is it fertile or poor? Are there trees in it or not?"'

Numbers 13:17-20

Moses sent twelve spies to explore the land. They were given a specific assignment – to explore everything from the land and soil to the towns and people. Moses wanted as much information as possible to enable him to have a full picture of the land they would inherit.

What was the response of the spies? Did they all come back with the same view?

'They gave Moses this account: We went into the land to which you sent us, and it does flow with milk and honey! Here is its fruit. But the people who live there are powerful, and the cities are fortified and very large. We even saw descendants of Anak there.... Then Caleb silenced the people before Moses and said, "We should go up and take possession of the land, for we can certainly do it." But the men who had gone up with them said, "We can't attack those people; they are stronger than we are." And they spread among the Israelites a bad report about the land they had explored. They said, "The land we explored devours those living in it. All the people we saw there are of great size... We seemed like grasshoppers in our own eyes, and we looked the same to them."'

Numbers 13:27-33

It appears there was a difference of opinion. Caleb saw the land differently from the other ten spies. He suggests they should take possession of the land. However, ten of the spies had a different perspective. They saw the milk and honey, however, they also saw the people, a people to be feared. The ten spies looked on the land through a lens of fear. Their lens made them feel they should stay away as they would be defeated if they went into Canaan. These ten spread their fear amongst the Israelites. How often are we influenced by others? How often have we looked through the lens that others are wearing rather than our own? How often have we been negatively impacted by many people saying the same thing? After all, they can't all be wrong, can they?

Of those that went to explore the land, ten looked at the land with a negative viewpoint; but there were two other spies: Joshua and Caleb. We have already seen that Caleb thought differently to the other ten. He looked through a positive lens and thought taking the land was possible. So, what about Joshua?

Joshua son of Nun and Caleb son of Jephunneh, who were among those who explored the land, tore their clothes and said to the entire Israelite assembly, 'The land we passed through and explored is exceedingly good. ***If the LORD is pleased with us,*** *he will lead us into the land, a land flowing with milk and honey and will give it to us. Only do not rebel against the LORD. And do not be afraid of the people of the land, because we will swallow them up. Their protection is gone,* **but the LORD is with us**. *Do not be afraid of them."'*

Numbers 14:6-9 (emphasis added)

Joshua had a different perspective from the other ten. Like Caleb, Joshua saw the land flowing with milk and honey, and he saw the occupants as a people who could be defeated. The key phrases Joshua declares are "*If the Lord is pleased*" and "*The Lord is with us*". For Joshua, he had a view that the other ten did not, he knew who God was. He was looking not through the lens of fear but through the lens of Heaven. He had seen God move before and was convinced of His ability and His power. The view of Joshua and the confidence he had in God was what set him apart from the ten. Notice God's response to this:

'How long will these people treat me with contempt? How long will they refuse to believe in me, in spite of all the miraculous signs I have performed among them?'

Numbers 14:11

Also notice:

'"...No-one who has treated me with contempt will ever see it. But because my servant Caleb has a different spirit and follows me wholeheartedly, I will bring him into the land he went to, his descendants will inherit it."... So the men Moses sent to explore the land, who returned and made the whole community grumble against him by spreading a bad report about the land were struck down and died of a plague before the LORD. Of the men who went to explore the Land, only Joshua son of nun and Caleb son of Jephunnah survived.'

Numbers 14:23b-24 and 14:36-38

Of the twelve spies, only two survived and inherited the land they explored. It was their faith in God that caused them to see differently. It was a belief that He was bigger. Yes, they saw the people of the land, but they also saw God. They had a history with God that enabled them to see from His perspective. So how did they see from His perspective? Let's go back to Exodus, to discover the history that Joshua had with God, and how he had a heavenly perspective on what he saw.

'The LORD would speak to Moses face to face, as a man speaks to his friend. Then Moses would return to the camp, but his young assistant ***Joshua son of nun did not leave the tent****.'*

Exodus 33:11 (emphasis added)

The tent of meeting was the place of God's presence and Joshua did not leave. It was the dwelling place of God. It was the place where Moses talked with God. Joshua remained in the tent as he had learnt to linger in the presence of God. He spent time in the tent of meeting and no doubt worship was on his lips. I think it was here that Joshua's relationship with God grew and I think it was here that Joshua began to see that God is good and faithful. I think it was here, in the tent, where Joshua learned what it was to follow Him completely. It was by remaining in that place that Joshua grasped something the other spies didn't. As a result, he was able to see things from a different viewpoint. He was able to look at the land and the people from the perspective of Heaven. He knew God, he had spent time with God and therefore he was not afraid.

Let's look at our life, and any prisons we are in, from the viewpoint of Heaven. Is there something we are not seeing? When we look from Heaven's perspective, we see with greater clarity. We can see those circumstances we face as they really are. What is Heaven's perspective of the prison you are in? What is your history with God? Is there something you can draw from which will enable you to begin to see from Heaven's perspective?

Whatever we are facing and whatever the prison we feel we are in, begin to look at it from the perspective of Heaven. As we to do that we will begin to see a way out.

Worship I

If you have been in and around church, you most likely will have seen people engaging in worship. However, worship doesn't just occur in churches, worship happens in different places. Worship happens in football stadiums, in cinemas, or music venues. Worship is more than singing songs, worship is an action. Worship is a choice we make. Worship is about lifting another higher than yourself. Some might, for example, worship a great football player or a Hollywood film star. We do this by having reverence or adoration for that person or thing which we are worshipping.

For Christians, worship is about lifting Jesus high. Worship is about honouring and giving praise to the One who is worthy. Worship is literally giving worth-ship. Worship is giving something of worth to the King. Worship connects the heart of the believer to the heart of the Father.

Worship doesn't have to be with spoken words, although it can help us, but rather worship is the devoting and surrendering of yourself in the presence of the Living God.

Worship is a key to being set free from our prisons. We see in Acts 16 that Paul and Silas were on their way to pray and were met by a slave girl who kept shouting at them. They commanded the demon influencing her to leave and she was set free. This resulted in Paul and Silas being stripped, beaten and locked in an inner cell of a prison. We then read that:

'After they had been severely flogged, they were thrown into prison, and the jailer was commanded to guard them carefully. When he received these orders, he put them in the inner cell and fastened their feet in the stocks. About midnight Paul and Silas **were praying and singing hymns to God,** *and the other prisoners were listening to them. Suddenly there was such a violent earthquake that the foundations of the prison were shaken.* **At once all the prison doors flew open**, *and everyone's chains came loose. The jailer woke up, and when he saw the prison doors open, he drew his sword and was about to kill himself because he thought the prisoners had escaped. But Paul shouted, "Don't harm yourself! We are all here!"'*

Acts 16:23-28 (emphasis added)

Paul and Silas were doing what they knew to do - worship! It was as they worshipped that the prison doors flew open. Paul and Silas's situation was a challenging one! It would have been easy to have been fearful, self-pitying or resentful for the situation they found themselves in. They could have questioned what was happening and possibly even blamed God for their circumstances. And yet - they worshipped. Whatever your circumstances are, no matter what prison you are in, I encourage you to worship and give Him honour and thanks. Your choice to worship amidst your situation can begin to unlock your prison doors.

A lot of the Psalms are songs of praise, worship and thanksgiving. Let's have a look at Psalm 100:

> *'Shout to the Lord, all the earth. Worship the Lord with* ***gladness****; come before him with joyful songs.* ***Know*** *the Lord is God. It is he who made us, and we are his; we are his people, the sheep of his pasture. Enter his gates with* ***thanksgiving*** *and his courts with* ***praise****; give thanks to him and praise his name. For the Lord is good and his love endures forever; His faithfulness continues through all generations.'*
>
> *Psalm 100:1-5 (emphasis added)*

King David gives us some insights about worship in this Psalm and lays out some simple steps on a journey into worship.

Gladness

The first step is to worship with gladness. The word for gladness is 'yadah', which means to throw off, but also to acknowledge or to confess.[30] Gladness also means to be joyful and to take pleasure and delight. More than that, gladness is a form of happiness.[31] Therefore, when we are glad, we can be joyful and happy. Happiness can also have a sense of contentment associated with it.[32] Maybe you're thinking "*I don't feel joyful, let alone content*". When you don't feel glad you might question "*if*

---

[30] Nelson Study Bible, (1997) NKJV. Nashville. Thomas Nelson Publishers
[31] https://www.vocabulary.com/dictionary/gladness (accessed March 2024)
[32] https://www.vocabulary.com/dictionary/happiness (accessed March 2024)

one of the steps in worship is gladness, then how can worship be a key out of the prison I find myself in"? Paul, as we read in Acts, was chained up in a physical prison. Paul's choice to worship suggests that we can still be glad and rejoice despite challenging circumstances. Paul writes in Philippians:

"I am not saying this because I am in need, for I have learned to be content whatever the circumstances…. I have learned the secret of being content in any and every situation, whether well fed or hungry, whether living in plenty or in want."'

Philippians 4:11-12

We know Paul spent time in prison and endured beatings and floggings. We can see from the verse above that he experienced times of hunger, yet still he says he has learnt to be content. So, what was Paul's secret? Let's read a few verses earlier in this chapter:

'Rejoice in the Lord always. I will say it again: Rejoice!'

Philippians 4:4

I think Paul's secret to being content in difficult circumstances was rejoicing in who God is. The root meaning of gladness *"simha"* is to be able to rejoice[33]. When we rejoice in Him, we put our focus on Him, which in turn causes us to be glad. When we rejoice, we take pleasure in what we are rejoicing in, which leads to being content. Therefore, we can take pleasure and be content in Jesus.

---

[33] https://www.blueletterbible.org/lexicon/h8057/niv/wlc/0-1/ (accessed March 2024)

Know the Lord is God

When life is challenging, sometimes it can feel difficult to truly 'know' in our hearts that He is Lord over our situation. Knowing the Lord is God here means to know by experience, or to recognise and understand.[34] We saw that gladness is linked with confessing or acknowledging. Paul teaches that if we confess with our mouth that Jesus is Lord, then we will be saved (Romans 10:9). The original word for saved used in this verse in Romans is the Greek word *sozo*, which means more than being set free from our sin. It means to be saved, healed and delivered. In other words, our entire being, spirit, soul and body can experience freedom and wholeness. So, as we confess with our mouths who Jesus is, we can know Him properly, and we can experience the fullness of who He is. We can experience the truth of who He says He is and His nature and characteristics. We recognise His Lordship in the circumstances of life we face.

I like the Passion Translation's phrasing of this verse:

'And realise what this really means – we have the privilege of worshipping the Lord our God.'

Psalm 100:3 (TPT)

We have the honour and privilege to come before the One who has won everything for us. When we come with this heart attitude then we truly know He is Lord, we come in worship.

---

[34] https://www.blueletterbible.org/lexicon/h3045/niv/wlc/0-1/ (accessed March 2024)

Thanksgiving

Let's look at the third step - thanksgiving. I look at thanksgiving in the Palace section of the book (chapter 18), but let's take a brief look at thanksgiving here.

Simply put, to be thankful is to be grateful for something.

It's easy to be thankful when we are enjoying life, or something good happens. For example, at Christmas or birthdays, if we receive the present we wanted, we express our thanks and gratitude to the one who gave it to us.

The original Hebrew word for thankfulness is *todah,* which means "thanksgiving offering", which is to express thanks to God. Thanksgiving and knowing who He is, is a route to gladness. Therefore, we can take our eyes off that which hold us back or entangle us by giving thanks and declaring God's goodness.

I find it helpful to start by thanking God for who He is and for something He has done. You can thank Him for His love for you, you can thank Him for the cross. Thank Him that He chose to die for you so that you might have life. Thank Him for His shed blood. Thank Him for His unchanging nature. Thank Him for His goodness. Thank Him for answered prayer. If nothing else, let these truths become ingrained in your heart and your spirit. Let these truths begin to influence your thoughts and attitudes. As these realities impact the way you think, you will begin to see the situations and circumstances through these truths.

Sometimes I find it helpful to ask Him to also bring to remembrance what He has done. As you thank Him for what

He has done you may remember other things He has done. Perhaps you have been healed, or you have heard a testimony of a healing – thank Him for that. Whatever you thank Him for, as you continue to thank Him, you'll begin to feel gladness and rejoicing enter your heart.

Praise

King David teaches that our thanksgiving is a gateway to praise (Psalm 100:4).

As we give thanks for what He has done, we can then begin to praise Him for who He is. When we praise Him, we begin to honour and acknowledge Him. Thanksgiving opens the doorway for praise.

Praising God for who He is, is about recognising His nature. He *is* majestic. He *is* holy. He *is* mighty. He *is* King. He *is* Lord. These are just some of the unchanging characteristics of who He is. It doesn't matter how we feel, what we're thinking or what we're going through. Who He is remains the same. He is the only one who can truly be dependable. Our situations and feelings may change. He never changes.

Notice that we enter His courts with praise. According to the Old Testament, people offered a sacrifice at the point of entering the courts (Leviticus 17:5). So, what is a sacrifice? For the people of the Old Testament, the sacrifice was an atonement for sins to receive forgiveness. The writer of Hebrews says:

'…without the shedding of blood there is no forgiveness.'

Hebrews 9:22

These offerings were typically animals, but they were costly. For us, sacrifice is about giving up something. In other words, it is about giving something of ours that is of value to the Lord.

The writer of Hebrews teaches us that our praise is a sacrifice:

'Through Jesus, therefore, let us continually offer to God a sacrifice of praise.'

Hebrews 13:15

Our praise should be a sacrifice; it should cost us something.

The writer of Hebrews said:

'…so Christ was sacrificed once to take away the sins of the people;…'

Hebrews 9:28a

Then we read a few verses later:

'The law is only a shadow of the good things that are coming – not the realities themselves. For this reason it can never, by the same sacrifices repeated endlessly year after year, make perfect those who draw near to worship.'

Hebrews 10:1

Jesus became the sacrifice. We have been made perfect by Jesus' one sacrifice (Hebrews 10:14). Therefore, because of His sacrifice we can be thankful, which leads us to be able to praise Him.

When we are thankful, we use our minds to remember what He has done. I think this in turn then opens the way for praise and as we do that, we use our spirit. As we take part in the first two, thankfulness and praise, we can then truly come to Him in worship. When we have thanked Him for what He has done and praised Him for who He is, we can worship Him in spirit.

Worship

Worship is about relationship, devotion, and intimacy. As we worship our spirit becomes more aware of the Holy Spirit. John encourages us to worship in spirit and truth (John 4:24). In other words, our worship should be genuine and authentic. When we worship in truth, we worship Him, not for what we may receive from Him, but simply because of who He is.

True worship includes being thankful and praising Him. True worship is about putting Him first. True worship is ministering to Him, loving Him and offering our adoration to Him.

'Does the Lord delight in burnt offerings and sacrifices as much as in obeying the voice of the Lord? To obey is better than sacrifice,…'

1 Samuel 15:22a

When we obey Him and choose to worship Him irrespective of what we receive, this action of obedience is a sacrifice. We choose to fully submit to Him. We are worshipping Him despite our circumstances. As we do this, we will see Him in His majesty and then we surrender, or sacrifice ourselves, because nothing else matters.

Worship is about recognising what He has done (thanksgiving) and who He is (praise). When we do that, we are in a place of being abandoned to Him, and then surrendering ourselves. When we are willing to give Him those things that hold us back and imprison us; and as we lay these at the cross, it allows us to be able to walk free. It becomes easier to deafen our ears to the lies of the enemy or as the Psalmist writes:

'You have built a stronghold by the songs of babies. Strength rises up with the chorus of singing children. This kind of praise has the power to shut satan's mouth.'

Psalm 8:2 (TPT)

There is power in our worship. Our worship has the power to shut the mouth of the enemy. As we worship and silence the lies of the enemy, our ears become more open to hear from Heaven. When we hear from Heaven, we can begin to walk free from those prisons that held us back. We have the power within us by the Holy Spirit, we hold the key to our freedom. The key is worship.

God is attracted to our worship. I think when we worship it invites more of the supernatural interventions of God. When He moves and when He acts, this increases our faith. Faith is not a prerequisite for Him to move but when He moves, it propels us into greater faith and greater thankfulness and praise.

Finally, King David encourages us:

'Lift up a great shout of joy to the Lord! Go ahead and do it – everyone, everywhere!'

Psalm 100:1 (TPT)

Make a choice today to silence the voice of the enemy. Make a choice today to worship Jesus. Make a choice today to recognise who He is. Make a choice today to look to Him and not your situation.

He *is* worthy of our worship!

Part 3
Palace

Palace

My hope is that as you have been reading this book, you've been encouraged and hope has been stirring within you that you *can* be free, and live in the palace. I hope you feel more empowered to use some of the keys to freedom that I have looked at. These keys are available to each of us to use as we transition to live in the palace.

Once we have taken up residence in the palace, who would ever want to go back to a prison? Who would willingly leave the palace; the place of His goodness, hope, the place of true identity and security? No one.

What is the Palace?

Living from a palace perspective is multi-faceted. Part of it is truly knowing who we are; seeing ourselves as the Father sees us. I believe the palace perspective is a mindset, a way of thinking. When we live from a palace perspective, we are able to see the way Jesus does. Living with a palace mindset means we have hope instead of hopelessness. We know we are valued and special instead of feeling worthless. We feel loved instead of feeling unloved. Troubles in life are unavoidable, but Jesus doesn't want us to be constrained by them, He intends for us to be overcomers. Therefore, having left the prisons, we *are* able to live free. Yes, we might be triggered, something might happen that causes us to feel imprisoned again, but we have a new mindset, we are able to see things the way Jesus does. The palace is our safe, secure home, as beloved sons and daughters living in intimacy with our perfect Heavenly Father.

The enemy however, doesn't stop trying to make us feel like we are back in the prison. He doesn't think "*Oh no, they've made it to the palace, I'll stop trying to influence or distract them now.*" No. He continues to do what he can to bring us back to a prison. He wants to bring us back to a place where we feel we aren't living in freedom and where we're held back by feelings linked to a prison. The prisons are a place of darkness and hopelessness - but the palace is a place of hope, light, freedom and purpose. The palace is the opposite of the prison. If we have reached the palace, surely there must be a way to stay there.

Let's not be like the Israelites who grumbled so much they wanted to go back to the place of captivity.

"Why is the LORD bringing us to this land only to let us fall by the sword? Our wives and children will be taken as plunder. Wouldn't it be better for us to go back to Egypt?" And they said to each other, 'We should appoint a leader and go back to Egypt.'"

Exodus 14:3-4

The Israelites had made it out of their prison (Egypt) and were on their journey to freedom. Yet they had lost sight of the slavery they endured in Egypt. They had forgotten that Egypt was not a place of freedom. They'd experienced challenges on their journey to freedom, they had seen the giants that appeared unbeatable. All they could see was the problem which appeared to them to be worse than the place they had come from. This is how satan wants us to feel. He hopes that we get so downcast by something, so distracted by an old way of thinking, that we instinctively fall back into prison thinking.

But - there is good news! There *is* a way to stay living in the palace; there is hope. It might be a battle, but it is one that we can win. It is possible to overcome!

Paul teaches us in Ephesians:

'For our struggle is not against flesh and blood, but against the rulers, against the authorities, against the powers of this dark world and against the spiritual forces of evil in the heavenly realms.'

Ephesians 6:12

Our struggle is not with people; it's with the devil. A friend of mine says "*The problem is, that often the enemy comes wrapped in flesh and blood.*" The enemy wants us to think we're fighting against other people, we therefore begin to blame others. The truth is these negative feelings that come to entrap us are not ours. Therefore, as a result, we *can* defeat them. The reality is we already live from a place of victory and hope.

'This is what the LORD says to you: 'Do not be afraid or discouraged because of this vast army. For the battle is not yours, but God's.'

1 Chronicles 20:15

Take heart because God *is* with us, and He fights for us! What battle has He not won?

Our thoughts might fluctuate, and we might feel like we're reverting to prison thinking, but your heart does not - your heart is still living within the palace. The enemy wants to bring you back to feeling locked up in the prison. Once we have lived in the palace, we have the keys in our possession to be able to go back to the palace even when we feel trapped again. The journey is easier. Now we know the route, we know how to use the keys. Yes, there might be a new diversion along the way, but we now know how to get to our destination.

I remember when my wife and I first moved to Milton Keynes. It's a city of many roundabouts. At first it appeared easy to get lost because the main roads in the city looked the same. Then someone gave us good advice and explained the best way to navigate around the city. Once we knew the 'keys', the best way to get from A to B, we no longer needed to rely on a satnav. The journey was much easier, even if a road was shut, we knew alternative routes. The keys you have make it easier to navigate your way back to palace living.

When we've experienced life in the palace but begin to encounter the old struggles, it might feel like we have a foot in both camps; a foot in the palace and a prison. We need to believe that having both feet back in the palace is possible. After all, it is the place we are living from anyway. We have the choice whether we go back to prison thinking or we continue to think as a resident of the palace. Occasional thoughts don't mean we're back in that same prison, however, if we allow the lies of the enemy to dominate our thoughts then we could end up thinking, once again, from a prison mentality.

In this third and final part of the book, I will look at some ways to help us continue to live in the place God would want us to live from - the palace. For now, though, let's look at some simple steps that can help.

We need to recognise that any struggles which hold us back do not define us. It is not who we are. Our thinking needs to align with the truth of who God says we are.

Having a prison mindset I believe, will hold us back. It is not conducive to living in the palace. Thinking the opposite of how God thinks about us is not helpful to living free and being the overcomers we are created to be.

Or as John writes:

> *'You see, every child of God overcomes the world, for our faith is the victorious power that triumphs over the world. So who are the world*

conquerors, defeating its power? Those who believe that Jesus is the Son of God.'

1 John 5:4-5 (TPT)

Living from a palace perspective allows us to identify more quickly the prison mindset we are starting to believe again. It becomes easier to not let those old thoughts influence us and therefore we can identify God's truth and live from that secure place – the palace!

The palace *is* the place we truly live from. I pray that as you read the following chapters you will be empowered to live a life of freedom, the life you were created to live.

'Let me be clear, the Anointed One has set us free – not partially, but completely and wonderfully free! We must always cherish this truth and stubbornly refuse to go back into the bondage of our past.'

Galatians 5:1 (TPT)

Know Who You Are

In order to live from a palace mindset, I believe it's important that we know who we truly are. I'm not talking about our giftings or our talents, although these things are important. I'm also not talking about our jobs or family roles. These are also important, but we shouldn't be defined by them. I am talking about a much deeper reality. I am talking about who God has made us, how He see us and our identity in Him.

For decades I didn't have a revelation of what this meant for me personally. I knew as a fact or a piece of information who God had made me. Yet it hadn't become a transforming revelation in my heart. When these truths move from mere head knowledge to revelation truths in our hearts, we can begin to experience them and we don't need to be limited by our old way of thinking anymore. We can then begin to walk in the freedom God has for us.

The Bible has much to say about who we are, who God has made us to be. However, it can be easy to gloss over familiar passages without really pausing to meditate on them. These words have life inside of them - they have the power to transform our beliefs and thought patterns. I firmly believe that when we have a firm foundation of the truth of who we are in Christ, it becomes a catalyst for overcoming the lies of the enemy. We can live more easily from a place of secure identity, with a palace mindset.

In this book I have covered some keys I believe can help us live a life of freedom. I think knowing who we truly are is one of the most fundamental ways we can live with a palace mindset. Knowing who we really are is our greatest defence against our enemy. The devil knows only too well that our true identity is worth him fighting for. You don't have to watch the television for too long before you are faced with identity related issues - people trying to answer the question of who they are. The devil has made it his mission to confuse, distort, and complicate our thinking. He tries to make people focus on the lie he is portraying and subsequently question their identity. He attempts to distort the truth. For example, in the garden of Eden he asked Eve "*Did God really say*?" (Genesis 3:1) He causes us to question what God says. He knows that if we listen to him, it can keep us locked up in the prisons. However, what God says about us is true! We have hope. As the truths of who we are transform us, we leave the prisons behind and live in the palace.

I've written much about our identity in my book 'In His Image: Rediscovering Who We Are' but I want to look at some of the truths about who we are in this chapter. As you read through these truths, I encourage you to meditate on them. As you meditate, listen to what God says to you personally about a specific truth. You might find it helpful to declare them out loud. When we speak out the truth, we are proclaiming them in faith that we will begin to believe them. This begins the process of the truth growing from simply a fact we know in our minds to becoming a heart revelation.

When I began to slip into thinking from a prison mindset again about my identity, I would speak out loud what I knew to be true. I knew the feelings and emotions I was struggling with were rooted in lies from the enemy. As I began to speak out the truths and listen to what God said, my thinking came back into alignment with God's truths. I was able to once more live with a renewed mind and live with a palace perspective. The enemy began to retreat because his lies were being drowned out by the truth. It's a daily process, but a process that really will shift and renew your thinking.

In the previous section about the keys, I looked at renewing our minds. I pray that as you read the following pages and truths from His Word, revelation will begin to transform your thinking, and you will begin to walk into greater freedom.

'Now it's time to be made new by every revelation that's been given to you.'

Ephesians 4:23 (TPT)

Created in His Image

Let's start at the beginning and remind ourselves that we *are* made in the image of God and what this means to us.

'So God created man in his own image, in the image of God he created him; male and female he created them.'

Genesis 1:27

We are created in His image – this is very significant! We are designed to bear His nature, to demonstrate who He is to those around us. God didn't create us to be like Him because He had no other plan. It was *the* plan! According to the creation story, He made the birds of the air and every living creature (Genesis 1:20-23) before He made mankind. At this point creation is described as "*good*" (Genesis 1:25). However, when God created man He described man as "*very good*" (Genesis 1:31). It stands to reason then that being made in His image is distinct and different to that of the rest of creation. When the Bible makes a statement like this it has a deeper meaning. God is saying we can reflect Him.

'As He is so we are in the world.'

1 John 4:17 (NKJV)

We can be like God to those around us - our work colleagues, our friends, our relatives, and our neighbours. Being made in His image simply means that we possess His nature. The nature of God is loving; therefore, we can be loving to those around us. His nature is to be kind; we therefore also have the power within us to demonstrate His kindness. God is good, therefore we should display His goodness to those around us. All the characteristics of His nature can be demonstrated to those around us by ourselves. When people look at us, they can see something of God in us. There have been many occasions when people have come into our home and commented on the peace they feel as they enter. Why? Simply because we honour His presence and His peace in our home. When Jesus says in John "*My peace I give to you*" (John 14:27) He is not just wanting that peace to remain with you, He wants it to be shared to those around us. Those who come into our home may not recognise it as the peace of God, but it is His peace nonetheless. We can reflect and release the nature of God to those around us.

Children Of God

The second aspect of our identity I want to look at is that we are children of God.

'You are all sons of God through faith in Christ Jesus.'

Galatians 3:26

This verse suggests the only requirement to be a child of God is to have faith in Jesus and what He did for us at the cross.

What a wonderful promise! Our right to be called children of God is not one we have to strive for or earn. It is ours by simply believing in Jesus. How many of us have felt that we had to do something as children to get the attention of our parents? Maybe you felt like you needed to get good grades at school? We don't have to strive or earn anything from Father God. We are His children!

Maybe you are reading this and asking, '*how does this affect me*'? Or "*this sounds too good to be true?*" Or you might be thinking '*if only you knew my life story*'.

There is however more good news, we read in Romans:

'And you did not receive the "spirit of religious duty" leading you back into the fear of never being good enough. But you have received the "Spirit of full acceptance," enfolding you into the family of God. And you will never feel orphaned, for as he rises up within us, our spirits join him in saying the words of tender affection, "Beloved Father!" For the Holy Spirit makes God's fatherhood real to us as he whispers into our innermost being, "You are God's beloved child!"'

Romans 8:15-16 (TPT)

Paul teaches us that we don't have to *feel* like we aren't good enough or that we must earn His approval. No. It's a done deal! We *have* His full acceptance. We are enfolded; we're completely wrapped up into the family of God. God is our Father. The New International Version says:

'And by him we cry, "Abba Father."'

Romans 8:15b

The use of the word 'Abba' indicates a close relationship; it implies affection and intimacy. There is no other closer relationship than that which we have been brought into with our Heavenly Father. We can call God our Father; we can call Him Daddy. That's who He is to us. He's not a distant Father or a Father that doesn't have time for you. He's a good and perfect Father (Matthew 5:48). He is for you (Romans 8:31). He is with you and will never leave you (Joshua 1:5).

Whether you already fully believe you are beloved child of God or not yet, I want to encourage you to start saying it over your life. Begin to repeat it day after day and watch the change this will make to the way you think. One time when I was driving home listening to a song, I kept hearing the phrase being sung "*I am a child of God*" over and over. It was like the CD was stuck on repeat of that line. By the time I got home about 30 minutes later, I can honestly say I noticed a difference. I felt as though the truth had penetrated my heart and I felt loved as a child of God.

Friend

The third aspect of who we are is a friend of Jesus.

'I no longer call you servants, because a servant does not know his master's business. Instead I have called you friends, for everything that I have learned from my father I have made known to you.'

John 15:15

Jesus is teaching His disciples here not to view Him as a master. The relationship between slave and master is very different to that of friends. The concept of having a master is one of giving up our freedom for another. The master has complete control over the servant's life. Instead, Jesus says He has a better life for us than that. He calls us friends. This description of the relationship suggests familiarity and a closeness. Love is the foundation of this friendship. In this passage Jesus is not describing Himself to His disciples as rabbi and disciple, but rather as a friend, one with whom we can trust and partner with. Unlike that of master and slave, a friendship is a relationship of closeness. It is a relationship based on love and freedom.

When we were growing up, some of us may not have enjoyed a good friendship group. Maybe you felt alone at school; maybe you were bullied or picked on? Know this - Jesus **is** your perfect friend. Love is the foundation of our friendship with Jesus; therefore, He cannot let us down or hurt us. Love is an integral part of the nature of God and He cannot act towards us in any way that is not loving. The Passion Translation uses the phrase "intimate friends" (John 15:15). What better love is there than to be intimate?

I've been on a journey of understanding what it means for me to have Jesus as my friend and brother. Over time I've come to realise that Jesus wants to have fun with us! He wants us to laugh and play together. It's like two best friends simply enjoying each other's company. I remember one time I saw a picture of Jesus playfully kicking water over me; He was smiling and laughing. These images might seem unholy to some. Let me ask you another question; what good friend wouldn't want to have fun with you? What good friend wouldn't want to laugh with you? A good friend has your best interests at heart. A good friend thinks of your needs, your likes and dislikes. A good friend knows what you need when you need it. Jesus is that good friend.

In 2017 I was sat with Jesus, and I felt Him say to me that He wanted to teach me what it is to have Him as my friend. Jesus said He wanted me to enjoy being with Him, as He enjoys being with me. He showed me that I hadn't always known what it was to have good friends, but that He wanted me to experience this aspect of my relationship with Him. He said to me that friends share things and talk to each other. He reminded me that often I had felt my friendships were one-sided. He said that His friendship is not like that, He said that true friendship is both ways. He said He wanted to listen to me and He wanted to talk to me. He said He was my best friend. There have been other occasions where Jesus revealed to me what it is to have Him as my true friend. Each time they have been full of love and full of acceptance. Whenever I have had a vision of our time together, we've had fun and played with each other.

My wife and I were once ministering to a lady who had never experienced Jesus as her friend. She had never thought that she could have fun with Him or that Jesus wanted to interact with her in this way. As she allowed Jesus to interact with her, we could see the delight and joy in her eyes. We could see this new revelation beginning to open her heart that Jesus is her friend.

We've seen that we are created in His image, that we are children of God and His friend. But there are more facets to who we are that we need to have heart revelation of, to help us remain living in the palace.

Loved

I've written a lot about God's love for us as His children and His friend. Let's look more closely at what the Bible teaches us about His love. I'll start with one of my favourite verses:

*'**Behold** what manner of love the Father has bestowed on us, that we should be called children of God!'*

1 John 3:1 (NKJV – emphasis added)

Or as the NIV phrases it:

'How great is the love the Father has **lavished** *on us, that we should be called children of God! And that is what we are!'*

1 John 3:1 (emphasis added)

As we read these two translations, I think we have some key words that help us to grasp the reality of these truths. The first is 'behold'. This means to look with amazement, to contemplate. To behold goes further, it's also about experiencing. The love our Father has for us is to be experienced.

The second word is 'lavished' which means to give out generously. The love Father has for us is so generous we are overwhelmed by it – we're unable to contain it. When we understand these two words, we begin to understand the depth of love Father has for each of us. The extent of the love from the Father is so great, so extravagant, that we would be amazed! As we meditate on the wonderous nature of His love for us we can begin to experience it too. Notice what happens as we do this, we realise we **already** are called His children. His love is so great that it shifts our perception of Him to enable us to see Him for who He really is. As this happens our understanding of what He feels about us becomes more aligned with the truth. His love for us is so amazing that it literally changes everything.

I encourage you to dwell on this truth and let the implications of it begin to open your heart and bring transformation to your thinking. As we dwell on it, it becomes almost impossible for the enemy to keep us in the prison. When we truly understand and experience this amazing love; when we appreciate that the God of the universe, the One who spoke creation into existence loves us with such an everlasting love (Jeremiah 31:3), then surely there is nothing that can keep us from living in the palace.

Rejoices over us with singing

We have begun to look at some amazing truths, but there's still more! As well as being made in the image of God, being children of God and friends of God - His feelings towards us don't stop there. His love for us is so great that He rejoices over us:

'The LORD your God is with you, he is mighty to save. He will take great delight in you, he will quiet you with his love, he will rejoice over you with singing'.

Zephaniah 3:17

I'm sure we've been at a sports match or watched a game on television and often all you can hear is the celebration and jubilation the supporters have for their team. The fans sing, rejoice, they dance and celebrate when their team is winning. Now, imagine that same scene in Heaven. Those scenes in Heaven are for you. Your Heavenly Father is delighted in you. He is so full of joy He simply can't stop expressing His pleasure over you. Maybe you are thinking "*but what about…*", or "*I don't deserve…*". Look at what the Amplified Version says:

'The Lord your God is in the midst of you, a Mighty One, a Saviour [Who saves]! He will rejoice over you with joy; He will rest [in silent satisfaction] and in his love He will be silent and make no mention [of past sins, or even recall them]; He will exult over you with singing.'

Zephaniah 3:17 (AMP)

The answer to your "*but what about...?*" is that He makes no mention of our past sins. They really are as far as the east is from the west (Psalm 103:12). No matter what question we may ask, He always comes back with "*I delight in you, I love you, I shout for joy over you.*"

His heart towards us is simple; He loves us. Therefore, begin to allow yourself to hear God's celebration over you. As the deafening sound of jubilation from Him cries out, the whispers of the enemy are drowned out. Tune your ear to Heaven. Tune your ear to the song the Father sings over you and you will find that is the only sound you can hear.

We've looked at just five aspects of who we are. I believe that as we meditate on these and declare them over ourselves, our minds will be renewed. We will begin to think about ourselves how Father God thinks about us. It is far more powerful to think what Father thinks about us than anyone else. His thoughts are true! As we think the same as the Father thinks, this helps us to remain living in the palace.

(In the Appendix I have listed other scriptures about what God says about us for you to meditate on).

Focus

I'm sure many of us have looked through a pair of binoculars to see the landscape or an animal far away. Perhaps you've looked through a telescope to see the moon in greater focus. Maybe you're a keen photographer, and you have a specialist camera that will give you the clearest picture. Most likely, the first time you looked through any one of these objects you had to adjust them to get the best focus in order to see clearly. It may have taken a few attempts, but eventually you were able to see with the clarity you expected.

There's been times when I've been driving on a motorway in the heavy rain and overtaken a lorry. As I overtake, I've been unable to see clearly. The windscreen wipers haven't been able to clear the screen quickly enough. In those situations it almost feels safer to stop, but I couldn't as that would have been dangerous. Instead, I just had to keep moving forward but slow down.

If a sprinter looks back during a race to see where the competitors are then they will at best slow down, but at worst they will trip and fall.

The enemy wants us to be distracted and focus on what he wants you looking at. The enemy wants us to stop altogether. However, if we stop, we're not moving forward, and then it is easier for him to cause us to look backwards. It's easier for the enemy to distract us, and for him to keep our eyes from being focused on the palace. The enemy wants us to focus on the wrong thing. We should be focusing on Jesus. The enemy wants us to look at where we have come from – the prison.

The writer of Hebrews says:

'Let us fix our eyes on Jesus the author and perfecter of our faith…'

Hebrews 12:2

We're encouraged to fix our gaze on Jesus, and not that which surrounds or entangles us. The Passion Translation puts it this way:

'We look away from the natural realm and we fasten our gaze onto Jesus who birthed faith within us and leads us forward into faith's perfection.'

Hebrews 12:2 (TPT)

When we look to Jesus we begin to focus on the realm of Heaven, and not the earthly realm. We begin to look to the One who holds all things in His hands (Colossians 1:17). When we focus on Jesus our perspective changes - we begin to see how He sees.

Have you ever looked at something in the distance, and then something catches your attention which is nearer, that object then comes into the foreground? That which is in the foreground always appears larger than what is in the background. What we focus on always appears bigger.

When our focus is on challenging life circumstances, or on the lies of the enemy, when our focus is not on Jesus, everything feels somehow distorted. It's like we're looking through a telescope without it being in focus. It appears that what we are focusing on is bigger than it is, it can look insurmountable. However - when we focus on Jesus; the One seated in heavenly places, the One who has all our situations and circumstances under His feet; we can begin to see through a wide-angle lens. We can clearly see the full picture. Before, all you could see was the circumstance. You were seeing a close-up of whatever you were focusing on. There appeared to be nothing else in the frame. Yet, when we begin to look at Jesus, then we can see more clearly - we can see the full picture. We can begin to see what Jesus sees. We can begin to see from His vantage point; from Heaven towards earth. From that vantage point the circumstance, situation, or problem no longer appear insurmountable. They can appear like a tiny spec from the viewpoint of Heaven. When we look from our position in the palace, what appeared to be a problem now appears insignificant in comparison to where we are sat.

Our situation and circumstances have changed from looking insurmountable to being possible to overcome. I encourage you to look at the situation, the circumstance, or the prison, through the lens of Jesus. Our focus become clearer looking through His lens.

The Psalmist encourages us to:

'Magnify the LORD with me; let us exalt his name together.'

Psalm 34:3

When we magnify something, we are making it larger. Have you ever used a magnifying glass and the item you are looking at appears to be much bigger than it is without the magnifying glass? The Hebrew word (gadal) used in this Psalm means to cause to grow, to make great or powerful.[35] Therefore to magnify the Lord helps us to recognise that He is great, and we see Him as greater than the circumstance or situation. Our faith in Him increases as we recognise that He is bigger and more powerful. When we magnify the Lord, we are choosing to focus with Heaven's perspective over the issue and therefore we are saying that God is who He says He is, despite the circumstance.

We've seen that we are seated with Jesus and can see life through from His lens. However, the enemy wants us to think we're back in the prison and seeing life from that viewpoint. In reality though, we are still in the palace and so we *can* see from that position. We may have been in a prison, but we have moved from that mindset to the mindset of the palace.

---

35 https://www.blueletterbible.org/lexicon/h1431/niv/wlc/0-1/ (accessed September 2023)

Let's take a look at the story of Job. Job was considered a man who feared the Lord. We read in the first verse of the book:

'This man was blameless and upright; he feared God and shunned evil.'

Job 1:1

Job's sole focus was the Lord, he loved God. He was blessed by God, "*he was, in fact, the greatest man amongst all the people of the east*" (Job 1:3). Job was innocent in the eyes of God. God Himself says of Job:

'There is no-one on earth like him; he is blameless and upright and fears God…'

Job 1:8

We read just a few verses later, that Job loses everything (Job 1:13-19). It doesn't stop there; it goes from bad to worse. We see in Chapter 2 Job develops sores all over his body (Job 2:7). It's at this point Job begins to receive 'helpful' advice from his wife. His wife says:

'Curse God and die!'

Job 2:9

Despite his wife's words, Job appears to remain focused on who God is. Job's response to his wife is:

"You are talking foolish woman. Shall we accept good from God, and not trouble?"

Job 2:10

Satan had tried to take Job's focus away from God through the attitude of his wife. When that failed, Job's friends appear and initially seem to be helpful. They acknowledge Job's pain and discomfort, and they sit with him and say nothing (Job 2:12-13).

This doesn't last long though. During the following 21 chapters Job's friends explain to him, how they think everything going wrong must be his fault (Job 4-25). When people who are close to us are discouraging, especially in difficult circumstances, we can easily take our focus away from God. We begin to look at the situation we are facing, or we begin to believe the lie of the enemy again. It's during these times we need to ensure our focus remains firmly on Him.

Job had one last friend, Elihu. In chapters 36 and 37 Elihu reminds Job of God's nature and greatness:

'How great is God – beyond our understanding'

Job 36:26

Job had been able find a voice, the voice of Elihu, who encouraged him to keep his focus on God and hear what God is saying. It is at this point that God begins to speak:

'Where were you when I laid the earth's foundations?'

Job 38:4a

What a way for Almighty God to start his conversation of Job. Job was a man who knew and feared God. I'm sure being asked this question alone would be enough for Job to come back to the place of focusing on God. Job wisely keeps listening and then responds:

'I know that you can do all things; no plan of yours can be thwarted. You asked, 'Who is this that obscures my counsel without knowledge?' Surely I spoke of things I did not understand, things too wonderful for me to know. You said, 'Listen now, and I will speak; I will question you, and you shall answer me.' My ears had heard of you ***but now my eyes have seen you.****'*

Job 42:2b-6 (emphasis added)

Job had come back to the place of looking at God. He looked away from his situation, he stopped listening to his friends, and satan's schemes were thwarted. Job gave his full attention back to the One he knows his life comes from.

We need to get to that place where we are looking at Jesus. When we have our focus set on Him, we can remain living from that palace perspective.

Focus on Jesus

Our focus should be on Jesus, and Him alone. It's easy to be distracted and focus on our situation rather than Jesus. When we focus on the wrong thing though, we can feel discouraged.

However - when we look at Him, and understand who He is and the power of His name, then we see more clearly.

Often when ending a prayer we say: "*In the name of Jesus.*" Why? It's a recognition that the name of Jesus, and therefore Jesus Himself, is the One who has all the power and authority. We are acknowledging that it is only Jesus that can change the situation we are praying about. Paul writes in Ephesians:

'And God placed ***all things*** *under His feet and appointed him to be the head over everything for the church, which is His body, the fullness of him fills everything in every way.'*

Ephesians 1:22-23 (emphasis added)

Notice the term "*all things*". That means everything! It means the situations you face now and the circumstances you may face in the future. It includes the lies about your identity which you may have difficulty with. It incorporates any shame, fear, or hopelessness you may have experienced. Everything!

The name of Jesus is the most powerful name in the universe. There really is power in the name of Jesus! I encourage you to meditate on His mighty power. As we begin to understand and believe this, the enemy will begin to run scared. The enemy does all he can to remind us of our past mistakes, or a prison we have left behind. But as we fix our full attention on Jesus, and all He accomplished, the enemy goes onto the back foot and starts to retreat. It is the person of Jesus; it is His name, that changes everything. His name represents all the finished work on the cross. It was Jesus that fulfilled God's plan of redemption and salvation. It was Jesus who won victory over sin and death. It was Jesus who broke the power of the kingdom of darkness and defeated the plans of the enemy. The verses before the ones we read a moment ago say:

'…and his incomparably great power for us who believe. That power is like the working of his mighty strength, which he exerted in Christ when he raised him from the dead and seated him at his right hand in the Heavenly realms, far above all rule and authority, power and dominion, and every title that can be given, not only in the present age but also in the one to come.'

Ephesians 1:19-21

The name of Jesus always carries power and authority. What a mighty name, the name of Jesus! He is to be worshipped, glorified and lifted high! We are to magnify and exalt Him! There is no other name in Heaven or on the earth which carries the same weight or significance. It is only the name of Jesus that has all the authority. There is no other name that can be compared to His mighty name. No king, no president or prime minister, has had the same influence as Jesus. No one else has had such a profound affect on Earth's history.

Do you still need a reason to focus on Jesus?

Over and over again in scripture we read of the effect Jesus had over situations, over sickness, even over death itself.

Let's look at just a few examples:

'The seventy-two returned with joy and said, "Lord, even the demons submit to us ***in your name.****'*

Luke 10:17 (emphasis added)

The demons were rendered powerless because of the name of Jesus. In the Gospel of Mark, we see Jesus declare:

'In my name they will drive out demons;…'

Mark 16:17b

Some translations use the phrase 'cast out'. This verse suggests that demons are deprived of all authority and influence[36] because they are driven away by His name. I love the phrase I heard Bill Johnson say: "*if Jesus has all the authority, the devil has none.*" Whatever circumstance you're facing right now that seems to have power or influence over you, look to Jesus and hide in the shadow of the Almighty (Psalm 91:1). Allow Jesus to drive away any demonic power that is influencing you.

In the next verse Jesus says about his followers:

'…they will place their hands on sick people, and they will get well.'

Mark 16:18

Peter and John in the book of Acts, experienced the power of Jesus' name:

---

[36] https://www.blueletterbible.org/lexicon/g1544/niv/mgnt/0-1/ (accessed November 2022)

'In the name of Jesus Christ of Nazareth, walk.'

Acts 3:6

The name of Jesus has so much power that just by speaking it aloud a lame man walked.

Finally, the greatest miracle of them all is found in the name of Jesus:

'Salvation is found in no one else, for there is no other name under Heaven given to men by which we must be saved.'

Acts 4:12

Salvation is only found in Jesus. There is an invitation for all to experience the power of His name:

'Everyone who calls on the name of the Lord will be saved.'

Romans 10:13

Whatever situation you may be going through, or whichever prison the enemy is trying to remind you of, keep your focus on Jesus and magnify His name. Are you feeling hopeless or disappointed? Are you feeling like your life has no direction? Are you feeling overwhelmed and stressed? Look to Jesus! Whatever it is, Jesus can intervene; He has authority over it. Build up your faith that His name is greater. Bring your focus back to Jesus and allow Him to influence you and your circumstances.

Jesus is our breakthrough! Let's join in with Heaven and declare how holy, how mighty, and how powerful the name of Jesus is.

'Therefore God exalted him to the highest place ***and gave him the name that is above every name****, that* ***at the name of Jesus every knee should bow****, in heaven and on earth and under the earth, and every tongue confess that Jesus Christ is Lord, to the Glory of God the father.'*

Philippians 2:9-11 (emphasis added)

The name of Jesus is above everything we face! Every knee, every situation, will bow to the name of Jesus. As you put your focus back on Jesus, let your situation bow to Him.

Thanksgiving

I'm sure we've all experienced being thanked for something we've said or done. How did it make you feel? Did it brighten your day? What about when you've thanked the cashier when paying for your items? How has the simple thank you made them feel? I have observed as I thank them, their face brightens.

What do you have to be thankful for? Are you only thankful when things are going well? Do you find it easy to be thankful while facing tough circumstances?

I think we find it easy to be thankful when something goes well, or when God answers a specific prayer. What about those times when it appears He hasn't? As I write this book the UK is facing some pressures; inflation is high, interest rates are rising, and many are finding it hard to balance their monthly income. What about in these times; can we be thankful then?

I remember many years ago I was in a worship meeting with thousands of people, and I found myself saying to God, I would worship Him in anything. I would worship Him in the good times, and I would worship Him in the bad times. This was easy to say in that moment; I was enjoying His presence in the worship setting and life was going well. Just a few months later the rubber hit the road. My mum was going into hospital for a major operation that the surgeons were confident she would recover from. The operation was successful, and she began her recovery. A week later we were called by the hospital to come in. Things were no longer looking good; my mum was only being kept alive by a machine and sadly we had to make the decision to turn off the life support machine. At that moment was thanksgiving first on my lips? Did I feel like worshipping the One who is worthy of our worship? I wasn't thankful my mum had passed away, and I had many weeks, if not months of grieving. There were painful times of missing her. Yet, I found coming to a place of worship and thanksgiving for who He is, was healing for my heart. In these times of worship I would easily cry. Was losing my mum hard? Definitely. Did I have questions? Absolutely. Did I want things to change? Certainly. Did I wish I could fast forward a few years, or rewind? Yes, I did. Did I blame Him? No. Through all the questions, however, one thing remained - Jesus was still my everything. He was still the One in whom I could depend.

We all go through seasons where being thankful isn't easy. We have circumstances where we wish things were different. However, as we'll see, giving thanks is something we should practice. No matter what we are facing, we all have something that we can be thankful for.

Whilst I was living in Malawi, I observed the Malawians were generally much quicker at giving thanks than I had observed in our British culture. In Malawi there aren't things in place to rely upon such as car breakdown cover or a reliable National Health Service. Therefore, you had to depend on God more than we might in the UK. As a result when something unexpectedly worked, we were thankful. I remember when we surprisingly had electricity for a whole day, instead of the scheduled 6 hours; we were very thankful!

I encourage you to develop a heart of thankfulness. Try and find something every day that you can be thankful for. I believe developing a heart of thankfulness is a way to remain living in the palace. Begin to thank Him for how He has brought you from the prison to the palace. Find verses that helped you, that you hold on to, and thank Him for them. As we stir our spirits with thankfulness our faith begins to rise, and our focus becomes more about Jesus and the enemy finds it harder to make us feel like we are back in the prison.

Testimony

No matter what prison you were locked up in, or if you feel you're struggling to maintain your rightful place in the palace, thank Him anyway. Thanksgiving is a recognition of what He has done, but it is also faith for what He is going to do. Thanksgiving is not just looking at the past, seeing where you have been and where you have come from. It's also a platform to propel us and move us forward.

The Book of Revelation says:

'Worship God. The testimony of Jesus is the spirit of prophecy.'

Revelation 19:10b (TPT)

When we give testimony, we're giving thanks for what He has done. This passage tells us that when we give thanks and share stories of what God has done, we are in essence prophesying '*Do it again*'. The word testimony literally means to '*do it again with the same power and authority*'. [37] When we speak out our testimony, we are opening the door for God to repeat what He has done. We are declaring God's goodness and faithfulness in times past, and we're opening the way for our hearts and spirits to remember what He did. We can be encouraged that if He did it once, He can and will do it again.

We read in Joshua 4:

'And Joshua set up at Gilgal the twelve stones they had taken out of the Jordan. He said to the Israelites, "In the future when your descendants ask their fathers, 'What do these stones mean?' tell them, 'Israel crossed the Jordan on dry ground.'"'

Joshua 4:20-22

The stones were set up as a reminder of what God had done for the Israelites and the story was passed down through the generations.

We read in Psalms:

---

[37] https://www.christianlearning.com/the-word-testimony-in-hebrew/ (accessed July 2024)

'One generation commends your works to another; they tell of your mighty acts. They ***speak*** *of the glorious splendour of your majesty and I will meditate on your wonderful works. They tell of the power of your awesome works and I will proclaim your great deeds. They* ***celebrate*** *your abundant goodness and joyfully sing of your righteousness.'*

Psalm 145: 4-7 (emphasis added)

Notice in this Psalm David is saying that we should speak of what He has done. We're being encouraged to share the stories of what He has done. As we tell others of the good news stories we have, we can celebrate and be thankful. When we do this our faith and hope rises that He can do it again.

I encourage you to write down your testimonies and remind yourself of them. I believe that where we have experienced a breakthrough in a particular area, then we shouldn't doubt in that area again. The breakthrough we've experienced should be our starting point if we encounter a similar situation again. I remember we were once trying to sell and buy a house. Our sale suddenly collapsed at a late stage. The builder we were buying from gave us 4 weeks to find a new buyer before he put the house back on the open market. We had testimonies of God working in our previous house sales and purchases, so we reminded ourselves of these. Doing this kept our focus on Him, and we found it easier to have faith He would do it again. We did find a new purchaser in those 4 weeks, and we were able to buy the house we felt God had for us.

Your testimony releases faith and hope into the spiritual atmosphere. When we hear other's testimony, it reminds us that

God is able and thankfulness rises up. Let's spend some time looking at what the bible says about being thankful.

Command

The first thing to notice is that thankfulness is a command.

'Be joyful always; pray continually; give thanks **in all** *circumstances, for this is God's will for you in Christ Jesus.'*

1 Thessalonians 5:16-18 (emphasis added)

Notice the key words '*in all*'. Firstly, Paul is not saying we should be thankful *for* everything. He is, however, encouraging us that we can be thankful *in* the circumstances. It's clear there are times, events, and situations in our life that don't warrant our thanks. I didn't thank God for my mum dying, but I was able to thank Him for my friends and remaining family; for how He sustained me, and the many other things I learnt during that time. Paul is also not suggesting we give thanks only when we feel like it. He's not saying when things are going well then that might be a good time to give thanks. We're being encouraged to give thanks in every situation. On the face of it this might appear easy to do. But when things are tough; when the enemy highlights things we can't be thankful for, in these times we might find it easy to gloss over this verse.

So - why should we give thanks in all circumstances? Paul tells us it's God's will. God *always* has our best interest at heart. He knows what is good for us. Giving thanks will help us. It helps us because as we give thanks, we are able to see Him for who He is. It allows us to take our eyes off the situation and look to God. The Passion Translation says:

'And in the midst of everything be always giving thanks, for this is God's perfect plan for you in Christ Jesus.'

1 Thessalonians 5:18 (TPT).

Notice again we're encouraged to give thanks '*in the midst of everything*'. Paul writes being thankful is part of God's **perfect** plan for us. It's impossible to improve on perfection. Perfect is the very best; it lacks nothing. Therefore, being thankful is one of the best things we can do. When we're going through difficult situations, let's give thanks for what He has done for us.

Having a thankful heart should be a high priority for us in our day-to-day life. Paul is encouraging us that **in** everything there is something that we *can* be thankful for. The act of giving thanks will propel us forward in faith as we fix our attention on what He has done and who He is. Giving thanks is an integral part of our Christian faith and life.

Choice

Is it possible for something to be both a command and a choice? Are they not opposite to each other? At a first glance the first two appear to be different.

Take for example a parent wanting their child to eat their vegetables. The parent knows the value of eating vegetables. Therefore, when the parents asks the child to eat their vegetables, they're pleased when the child eats them. How much more though, will the parent be thrilled when their child chooses to eat them willingly without being asked? A simple illustration to demonstrate that Father God tells us to be thankful in all things for our own good. We can be thankful because we know it's good for us, or, over time as we grow in this area our thankfulness becomes a natural overflow of our intimate relationship with Father.

Let's look at what the Bible says about choosing to give thanks:

'And when you offer a sacrifice of thanksgiving to the LORD, offer it of your own free will.'

Leviticus 22:29 (NKJV)

God knows it's good for us to give thanks. He knows when we choose to be thankful, that's even better! When we choose to do something (like giving thanks), it comes from the heart rather than a sense of duty. When something comes from our heart it comes from the very core of who we are. If we do something because we are told to, we might do it begrudgingly. We might be inwardly thinking "*I am only doing this because I am told to, I don't really want to.*" When we do something out of choice, we are pleased to do it. It has more significance to both the one giving thanks and the one receiving thanks.

Can I encourage you, if you don't feel like giving thanks right now, then do so because there is a command to do it, because it is good for you. It helps us remember that God has worked in our life, and in doing so enables us to turn our attention to what He has done. My experience is that as you give thanks, over time the attitude of your heart will change, and you choose to give thanks freely. The command is a great starting point which leads to developing a heart of thankfulness.

Lifestyle

As we move from following the command to be thankful to choosing to give thanks in everything, we then cultivate a lifestyle of thankfulness.

'Now when Daniel knew that the writing was signed, he went home. And in his upper room, with his windows open toward Jerusalem, he knelt down on his knees three times that day, and prayed and ***gave thanks*** *before his God, as was his custom since early days.'*

Daniel 6:10 (NKJV - emphasis added)

Daniel made giving thanks part of his lifestyle. This verse describes it as his custom. It was a rhythm of life.

Paul in his letter to the Colossians encourages us to be devoted to prayer and thanksgiving:

'Devote yourselves to prayer, being watchful and ***thankful.'***

Colossians 4:2 (emphasis added)

Devoting means to wholeheartedly persevere with being thankful. When we develop a lifestyle of thanksgiving, even in challenging circumstances, it becomes harder for the enemy to hold us in a prison. The enemy knows the importance of giving thanks. If thanksgiving becomes our custom, it becomes more difficult for satan to remind us of the past situations; because what God has done for us is always better. God's action trumps our actions. Having a lifestyle of thanks keeps us focused on God - on who He is and what He has done.

As we cultivate a lifestyle of gratitude and thanksgiving, eventually we do it without thinking. I tell my wife every day "*I love you*". Does it mean it has less meaning? No. It's a choice, a lifestyle I have created to tell her I love her. The more I tell her, the more I find things I love her for. The same is true of a lifestyle of thankfulness. The more we choose to create such a lifestyle the more we mean it, and the more we have to give Him thanks for.

Focus

As we make this choice to develop a lifestyle of being thankful, it becomes easier to not be distracted by the things the enemy wants us focus on. The Israelites in the Old Testament were often looking back, they were not always content with what they had (Exodus 16:2, Numbers 14:4). They had the mentality that '*the grass is greener on the other side*'. The problem was that when they were on the other side, they thought it was better where they were before, in Egypt, in slavery. They forgot what life was like back there.

'The rabble with them began to crave other food, and again the Israelites started wailing and said, 'If only we had meat to eat! We remember the fish we ate in Egypt at no cost – also the cucumbers, melons, leeks, onions and garlic. But now we have lost our appetite; we never see anything but this manna!'

Number 11:4-6

The Lord promised to feed the Israelites and He fed them manna from heaven. Yet they were not satisfied with what God was giving them. They continued to look back at what they had before whilst in captivity; the meat, fish and vegetables. It seemed like they'd forgotten they were forced to lives as slaves. They'd forgotten their living and working conditions (Exodus. 1:14). They appear to only remember the positives.

Often my wife and I reminisce about our time living in Malawi. We absolutely loved living there and count it a privilege to have done so. However, we often only seem to remember the good times. We seem to forget the stresses and challenges of living in a foreign land. We recognise we look back with rose tinted glasses of our time there.

So often we can look at what we don't have. The enemy wants us to look at the current challenge we're facing and will try to convince us that where we were (the prison) was better for us. As we develop a heart of thankfulness and focus on Him, we can begin to see the good and then we can begin to be thankful. When we're thankful the lies of the enemy will be silenced, and we will hear what God says. We will begin to experience the revelation of God's thoughts about us. We will begin to focus on the good and not the bad. We focus on the truth, not the lies.

Thankfulness is the enemy of sadness and frustration. Thankfulness can be the switch that turns darkness into light. Thankfulness can lead us to peace in the middle of the storm. Thankfulness is a key to remaining in the palace. When we're thankful, we begin to change our focus from the prison to the palace.

Contentment

When we cultivate a lifestyle of thankfulness and our focus begins to change, we can experience contentment, peace and happiness.

Let's remind ourselves, as we read earlier in chapter 14 what the apostle Paul says:

'I have learned to be content whatever the circumstances. I know what it is to be in need, and I know what it is to have plenty. I have learned the secret of being content in any and every situation.'

Philippians 4:11b-12a

Paul understood how to be content and he says there is a secret to it. Paul was in prison when he wrote this letter. He had suffered many beatings and his future was uncertain, yet he was able to write these verses. How many of us, whilst in our prisons, could write these words?

So, what was Paul's secret to being content? How was he able to write such encouraging words? The answer, I believe, is found a few verses earlier:

'Rejoice in the Lord always. I will say it again: Rejoice!... but in every situation by prayer and petition, with thanksgiving, present your requests to God.'

Philippians 4:4 and 6

When we give thanks, we can be joyful and rejoice as we do so. When we're thankful, we can become content in whatever circumstances we find ourselves. Our focus is not on the situation but on Jesus. Our contentment is not dependent on our circumstances, it is found only in Jesus.

The Passion Translation of this verse says:

'Be cheerful with joyous celebration in every season of life. Let joy overflow, for you are united with the Anointed One.'

Philippians 4:4 (TPT)

We are united and joined with Christ, the One in whom nothing is impossible (Luke 1:37). With this truth how can we not be thankful? How can we not be content in every circumstance? The circumstances and situations of life we face are nothing compared to Jesus. The prison of the lies of the enemy is nothing to Jesus. Do you want to be content? Look to Jesus!

Worship

As we learn to be content through our thankfulness, we can worship. We will look in the next chapter about the importance of worship, and the relationship between thankfulness and worship. However, as we choose to be thankful our hearts begin to turn towards Him, and this causes us to worship.

'Let us come before him with thanksgiving and extol him with music and song.'

Psalm 95:2

Thanksgiving turns to exaltation; to worshiping Him. As we give our thanks and remember what He has done for us we can't help but be drawn to worship Him.

'Since we are receiving our rights to an unshakable Kingdom we should be extremely thankful and offer God the purest worship that delights his heart as we lay down our lives in absolute surrender, filled with awe.'

Hebrews 12:28 (TPT)

We have a right to this unshakable Kingdom. Just like a Prince or Princess next in line to a throne, we have the rights to the Kingdom because we're co-heirs with Christ (Romans 8:17). Wow – that's something to be thankful for! The revelation of this truth should lead us to give Him all our thanks, and in turn, lead us to worship.

I love this testimony from Wendy Mann's book 'Naturally Supernatural: The Normal Christian Life':

"As the worship started, I was quickly aware of how tired people were around the room, the overriding atmosphere in the room could only be described as lethargic. That is until one of the students started to shout a prayer of thanksgiving to God. It was like something came alive in the student's heart as she declared truth after truth about God's nature. She thanked Him for His goodness, and His grace, His love and His kindness. Her prayer went on and on until she ran out of words to say. 'God, you're just brilliant!' was how her prayer ended. The atmosphere in the room went from lethargic to electric. The thanksgiving not only made something come alive in the students' heart, it made the rest of us come alive too. One prayer of thanksgiving resulted in a tangible rise of faith across the whole room. It was a powerful moment that had a significant impact on the rest of the evening." [38]

---

[38] Mann, W. (2015), Naturally Supernatural: The Normal Christian Life, p.105 (Permission granted)

Learn from Him

When we chose to make time and space in our lives to thanking Him, we begin to position ourselves to learn from Him. We can begin to see from His perspective.

If I have read a book that impacts me, I may thank the author. If I listen to a sermon that gives me fresh revelation, I thank the preacher. Other times I thank a person for simply being who they are. This opens the way for dialogue to take place, and I begin to hear the heart of the person whom I was thanking. When we thank someone, they respond. Recently I thanked someone for a short talk they gave. It was a great talk and there was something in it that caught my attention. As I thanked the lady, she began to share that she finds giving that type of message difficult. She described to me how she had stepped out of her comfort zone. Without my thanks to her, I would never have learned this about the lady, I would have assumed she found it easy.

The same is true of God. When we thank Him, it opens the way for conversation. It enables our heart to connect with His. Not only do we see something of Him, but as our hearts connect, we also learn something about ourselves too.

'Now on his way to Jerusalem, Jesus travelled along the border between Samaria and Galilee. As he was going into a village, ten men who had leprosy met him. They stood at a distance and called out in a loud voice, "Jesus, Master, have pity on us!" When he saw them, he said, "Go, show yourselves to the priests." And as they went, they were cleansed. One of them, when he saw he was healed, came back, praising God in a loud voice. He threw himself at Jesus' feet and thanked him—and he was a Samaritan. Jesus asked, "Were not all ten cleansed? Where are the other

nine? Has no one returned to give praise to God except this foreigner?" Then he said to him, "Rise and go; your faith has made you well."'

Luke 17:11-19

In this story ten men asked Jesus for healing. They were healed. However, of the ten, only one returned to thank Jesus. Notice, Jesus doesn't say "*Well done, you have done the right thing.*" or "*Go get your friends so they can thank me too.*" No. Jesus tells the man why and how he was healed. Jesus says, "*Your faith has made you well.*" In this simple transaction of thanks and gratitude the man learnt something about the heart of God. The man received more than his healing - he learnt something of the importance of both obedience and faith. He began to understand the role that faith played in his healing. Had the man not returned to give thanks he wouldn't have had this opportunity to learn from Jesus. When we thank Him, it opens the door to our receiving more from Him than the answered prayer. Thanking Him demonstrates we are interested in more than simply what we can receive from Him. We're wanting increased intimacy in our relationship with Him.

Victory

When we give thanks it can be a launching pad for breakthroughs in our lives. It *is* possible to thank Him for what He hasn't yet done!

Are you contending for healing? God is our healer; it is in His nature to heal. I was once praying for someone with a fallen arch in their foot. I'd been praying for a few minutes and nothing appeared to happening. As I was about to stop, I felt God say "*thank Me.*" As I enquired of the Lord, I felt like He said, "*Thank Me for the healing, even though you don't see it yet.*" I explained to the person what I felt led to do and spent the next minute or so thanking God for the healing. As I thanked God for the healing, the foot was healed! Through thanking God for the healing (which I was not experiencing or seeing), it released faith into the atmosphere and that faith resulted in the person being healed by Jesus. Paul teaches:

'But thanks be to God! He gives us the victory through our Lord Jesus Christ.'

1 Corinthians 15:57

Sometimes being thankful can bring the very breakthrough we need. We might feel disappointed for something that has not happened. We might stop looking to Him and start focusing on what we don't have. Remember - thankfulness changes our focus, but so too can being unthankful. It can cause us to start looking back and not forward. I want to encourage you to thank Him *before* you have seen the answer to your prayer. Has God forgotten His promise to you? No. Are you waiting for a promise of God to be fulfilled in your life? Thank Him. Every word that God speaks is always fulfilled. Take heart in this promise we looked at earlier:

'So is my word that goes out from my mouth: It will not return to me empty, but will accomplish what I desire and achieve the purpose for which I sent it.'

Isaiah 55:11

What a promise! His word is *always* accomplished. Rest on this promise and truth. This verse provides us with a stepping stone to a heart of thanks, even in times of needing a breakthrough. Notice the following verse:

'You will go out with joy.'

Isaiah 55:12a

When someone is full of joy, it's easier for them to be thankful. This passage in Isaiah encourages us to be joyful as we rest in that promise of God's fulfilled word. As we are joyful, be thankful. I think there's a link between thankfulness and breakthrough. We know God is faithful, therefore we *can* be thankful while we wait for our breakthrough to come into fruition.

Life

We've seen that cultivating a heart of thanksgiving is both a command and a choice. We've looked at having a thankful heart leads us to worship, which in turn change our focus. However, the reverse is also true. When we are not thankful, this can take our focus away from Him.

'Nor should there be any obscenity, foolish talk or coarse joking, which are out of place, ***but rather thanksgiving.****'*

Ephesians 5:4 (emphasis added)

The Passion Translation puts it like this:

'Guard your speech. Forsake obscenities and worthless insults; these are nonsensical words that bring disgrace and are unnecessary. Instead, let worship fill your heart and spill out in your words.'

Ephesians 5:4 (TPT)

Paul is saying that negativity and unhealthy words are out of place for believers. They don't bring us life. In the previous chapter Paul says "*don't let unwholesome talk come out of your mouth*" (Ephesians 4:29.). Have you ever been around someone who speaks negatively? How did it feel? What were you thinking as you have listened to their words? Negativity can breed negativity. Someone with a negative mindset will focus on the bad. These people can influence those around them to feel the same. I've been in environments where negativity is dominant; people are speaking negatively and before I know it, I begin partnering with those same feelings. As this has happened, it has often felt easier for me to leave the room. I know negativity is not good for me, it certainly has not brought me life. However, it is important to recognise what is happening and decide not to partner with the negativity, but instead speak life and hope.

Paul encourages us instead to have words of thanksgiving coming out of our mouths. Having a heart of thankfulness can affect our feelings and emotions and will begin to breathe life back into our spirits. If I'm around negativity I try and speak life or hope and focus on what we can be thankful for and my words change the atmosphere.

If we can develop a thankful heart our outlook and perspective will change. We'll begin to focus on the positive and we will begin to see life. Even if our circumstances don't change and we don't yet see the victory, our perspectives will still carry hope. I've prayed for people who haven't been healed. I've learnt that by remaining thankful for what God has done in them and encouraging them of how much God loves them, they walk away with hope and faith.

I want to encourage you to cultivate a heart of thanksgiving in all situations. As you do this, over time observe how your heart and attitudes change. As we cultivate a heart of giving thanks, we will begin to remain living in the palace. The enemy who speaks lies to discourage us will lose influence in our lives.

Everyday my wife and I find things from our day that we can be thankful for. It makes a difference to how we may be feeling, and we begin to focus on Him rather than what we don't have. I encourage you to be deliberate about developing a thankful heart. Make it a conscious choice and be purposeful. Look beyond your circumstances and begin to see them through a heart of thanks.

Worship II

We saw in Part 2 that worship is a key to walking out of our prisons and moving towards the palace.

In this chapter I want to go deeper and look at how worship isn't solely a key, but an important ongoing priority in our daily lives for remaining in the palace.

Once we have taken hold of the key of worship (chapter 14), I believe He wants us to linger for longer with Him in worship. He wants us to take our time and not rush on. I believe He wants each of us to dwell with Him. He has made it possible for each of us to come and rest in His presence in worship. I believe that by seeking His face and His presence and choosing to remain there, we can experience freedom and restoration. By abiding there, we can live from the perspective of the palace.

Once when I was battling in my mind to remain living from a palace perspective, I heard a line in a song '*Lift up your hallelujahs*'. I asked Father what this meant, and I sensed Him say to me "*Lift up your praise to Me*". As I began to praise to Him, my mind began to focus on Him, and my heart felt lighter. I realised that as we begin to praise Jesus and be thankful for who He is and what He has done, we become more aware of Him than the battles in our mind.

As we worship Him it takes our focus away from the circumstances that might seek to imprison us and puts our focus back onto Him. Worship is not something we only do when things are going well, it is something we do even during our challenges.

Wilderness

Sometimes we can see challenges as something we have to endure or get through. We might feel like God is distant from us; it could feel like we're in a barren place or a wilderness. In these times we may not feel like worshipping. God, however, wants to meet us in those places. The Israelites were instructed by God to build a tabernacle (a place of worship) whilst they were in the wilderness (Exodus 25:8). God knows the importance of worship. No matter what we're going through, He wants our worship.

The Hebrew word for wilderness *"midbar"* means God is speaking.[39] Let's take a moment to look at a passage in Hosea to get better understanding of this.[40] The book of Hosea is a love

---

39 https://rabbisacks.org/covenant-conversation/bamidbar/the-wilderness-and-the-word/ (accessed July 24)

40 I heard Paul Oakley teach on this in October 2022.

story; a story of how God wants to restore Isarel back to Himself.

'Therefore, behold, I will ***allure*** *her,*
Will bring her into the ***wilderness,***
And speak comfort to her. I will give her vineyards from there,
And the Valley of Achor as a door of ***hope;***
She shall sing there,
As in the days of her youth,
As in the day when she came up from the land of Egypt.'

Hosea 2:14-15 (NKJV – emphasis added)

God says He will bring her (Israel) to the wilderness. He allured her to that place. When we hear the word wilderness we might think of a dry, hard, even a lonely place. Why would a loving Father want to bring His people here? Let's remember, the wilderness is a place we can hear God speaking to us clearly. It can be a place of encounter. It can be a place where hope is restored. It was in the wilderness where Moses had an encounter with God in the burning bush (Exodus 3:1). God wants us to encounter Him and experience the freedom He has for us. As we encounter Him, we can live in that hope of freedom, in the palace.

God says in these verses He will speak comforting words in the wilderness. He wants to be with us in such a way, that there would be nowhere else we would want to be. God wants us to know when we feel like we're back in a prison, feeling like we're in a wilderness, He is **always** present and available to comfort us. As we seek Him, He will come near to us. (James 4:8).

The Valley of Achor mentioned in this passage means the place of troubles.[41] Even in our place of trouble, we can find hope. This passage describes the place of trouble transformed into a door of hope.[42] As we encounter Him, our troubles – which may make us feel like we're back in a prison, are transformed into a door of hope. An encounter with God can change our focus from troubles to hope. Let me encourage you, God wants you to encounter Him.

Encounter

We can encounter God in many ways. For me, I encounter God in worship. Worship can lead us into an encounter with Him which in turn shifts our focus from our troubles to hope, it leads us back from the prison to the palace.

I had a powerful encounter with God in August 2022. My life was transformed. I was at David's Tent; an annual 72-hour worship event in England. We (thousands of worshippers) were singing about the holiness of God over and over - then I sensed God tangibly enter the meeting. In that moment all I could do was kneel at His feet. Whilst on my knees I cried for the remaining hours of the evening. In fact, for the next two days, whenever I entered the worship tent all I could do was kneel and cry. In that moment nothing else mattered.

In those first few hours, I felt God say to me that all He has ever wanted was all of me. He said that as I give Him all of myself, then He gives me all of Him. As I give my everything: my

---

[41] https://www.blueletterbible.org/lexicon/h5911/niv/wlc/0-1/ (accessed July 2024)

[42] https://www.blueletterbible.org/comm/guzik_david/study-guide/hosea/hosea-2.cfm?a=864015 (accessed July 2024)

circumstances, my finances, my entire life, then in exchange, I receive all of Him.

I was struck by the magnitude of the exchange! I realised, maybe for the first time, how this exchange wasn't a fair one. How unfair it is that as I give Him myself, I receive the King of Kings. I get **all** He has to offer, all of Him! It's an exchange that Jesus made possible for us. I sensed He said that *He desired* that exchange. Even if we give Him our everything - without Jesus we cannot receive all that He is and all that He has. Father God gave Jesus before I gave of myself. Jesus sacrificed everything for me - why wouldn't I want to give Him everything in return?

I realised this was a life-changing revelation. It changes everything - forever! I knew that if I was to fully grasp what this means then Jesus *must* become my everything. He must be the sole reason I am alive. Now, with this revelation, whenever I go through challenging times, they become nothing compared to who He is. Nothing else will suffice. Only Jesus will satisfy. We need to come to that place where only He satisfies us; where He becomes our everything and we choose to focus solely on Him.

On our Knees

Even after such an intense encounter, I'm still on the journey of Jesus truly being my everything and sole focus in life. I've become convinced the best place we can be is at the feet of Jesus. We come to the feet of Jesus on our knees. True worship is loving God with all our heart; loving Him with everything we have and everything we are. We bow before Him on our knees at His feet. Being on our knees is a posture of sacrifice, abandonment and humility. It is a place of obedience, vulnerability and emptiness, where we give all that we have to

Him. This attitude is nothing in comparison to what Jesus sacrificed and endured for us. Jesus' suffering was His choice. He chose to give up His life for you and me. Therefore, He deserves our everything. He wants us to choose to come to Him on our knees and sacrifice all we have to Him.

At the feet of Jesus

During this 3-day encounter on my knees at His feet in tears, Jesus said to me "*Your tears are like a sacrificial oil being poured out, anointing me. Let My hair wipe your tears away. As I do this, it creates space for more tears. Let more come. It is so beautiful watching you sacrifice to Me and being abandoned to Me.*" I sensed Jesus wiping away my tears. I then saw Jesus come off His throne, get on His knees next to me and then wrap me in His robe.

I want to encourage you to be hungry to worship Him. To be so in awe of Him that the only place you want to be is at His feet.

Being at the feet of Jesus is a place to discover the goodness of God. When we are at the feet of Jesus, we focus on Him and become even more aware of who He is, and therefore not on our circumstances. Being at the feet of Jesus is a place of hope, a place of victory and triumph.

Being at the feet of Jesus is a way to overcome, a way out of the prison way of thinking and enables us to posture our hearts back into palace thinking. When we're at the feet of Jesus it fixes our focus back on to Him.

Do you want to see the goodness of God? Being at the feet of Jesus is a great place to start. When we rest at the feet of Jesus, we can experience peace, hope, comfort and perspective.

Resting at the feet of Jesus brings change. Resting at the feet of Jesus brings the answer - Jesus is the answer.

As we come on our knees to the feet of Jesus, as we surrender to Him, as we give everything we have to Him, then our circumstances, our worries, and our problems come under His feet.

Footstool

During this encounter I had at the feet of Jesus, He also spoke to me about a footstool. What is a footstool? A footstool could be described as a footrest. It's simply a place of rest. In the Bible it depicts a place of victory.[43] Let's look at what this means in the context of remaining in a palace mindset.

The Psalmist writes:

'The LORD (God) says to my Lord (the Messiah), sit at my right hand, until I make your adversaries your footstool.'

Psalm 110:1 (AMP)

Our adversary, the enemy, uses our unhealthy mindsets and lies we believe, to keep us locked up away from the palace. However, these are a footstool for Jesus. He has victory over them. He has conquered them. They are in complete submission to Him. Paul writes:

[43] https://forwardinchrist.net/jesus-enemies-footstool/ (Accessed July 2024)

'And God placed ***all things*** *under his feet and appointed him to be head over everything for the church.'*

Ephesians 1:22 (emphasis added)

I want to be clear here, there is often a process to changing old mindsets, after all they have often been formed over many years. The enemy uses these mindsets to try to keep us locked up, but notice in this passage it says "*all things.*" This is clear - it means everything. Anything that has ever existed that sets itself up against Christ, including those negative mindsets that we struggle with, are **all** under His feet. No matter how we may feel, this verse remains true, they are under Jesus' feet. His enemies are a footstool to His feet (Luke 20:43). For something to be under Jesus' feet means that He has conquered it. He has subdued it and has overpowered it. Jesus rules over it. It is defeated.

When we sit with Jesus, we rest and stop striving. As we sit with Jesus, we can place our difficulties and problems at His feet; they become a footstool for Him. We can rest on the very things that seek to give us unrest. There is victory that can be had, when we rest with Jesus.

Isaiah writes:

'Heaven is my throne, and earth is my footstool. Where is the house you will build for me? Where will my resting place be?'

Isaiah 66:1

God is inviting us to build a resting place for Him. How do we do this? I think the house He refers to here is our hearts. When our hearts are full of love and worship, and adoration of Him, then our hearts become His resting place. As He fills our hearts and minds, we too find rest and peace.

Jesus says:

'Come to me all who are weary and burdened, and I will give you rest.'

Matthew 11:28

I think complete rest looks like handing over everything, all of our cares and struggles, worries and fears, to the one who promises us rest - Jesus.

Where there is rest, striving ceases and worry and doubt subside. Rest and striving cannot co-exist with each other.

I think we can try to overcome problems through our own efforts. Yet in our efforts to overcome these problems, we ourselves become overcome. However, as we bring these to Jesus, then He overcomes them, and we find rest. Worship can bring us to a place of rest.

Let's have a look at when Jesus visited the home of Mary and Martha:

'… He [Jesus] came to a village where a woman named Martha opened her home to him. She had a sister called ***Mary, who sat at the Lord's feet*** *listening to what he said. But* ***Martha was distracted*** *by all the preparations that had to be made. She came to him and asked, "Lord, don't you care that my sister has left me to do the work by myself? Tell her to help me!" "Martha, Martha," the Lord answered, "you are*

worried and upset about many things, but few things are needed – or indeed only one. Mary has chosen what is better, and it will not be taken away from her.'"

Luke 10:38-42 (emphasis added)

We see two sisters operating out of two different places. Martha was worried and distracted (Luke 10:40), but Mary sat at His feet (Luke 10:39). Notice what Jesus says to Martha about Mary:

'*... but only one thing is needed. Mary has chosen what is better...*'

Luke 10:42

Jesus is explaining to Martha that Mary chose the most important thing. She chose to be sat at His feet, rather than be busy 'doing' whilst in the presence of Jesus.

Let's read a few of these same verses from The Passion Translation:

'Martha, my beloved Martha. Why are you upset and troubled, pulled away by these many distractions? Are they really that important? Mary has discovered the one thing most important by choosing to sit at my feet. She is undistracted, and I won't take this privilege from her.'

Luke 10:41-42 (TPT)

I imagine Martha being pulled away from Jesus by making sandwiches no one ordered. She was distracted. Mary on the other hand remained undistracted. Mary discovered the one thing. The best thing - the resting place at Jesus' feet. Martha was not at rest; Mary was at rest. Martha had a 'to-do list', Mary was doing one thing – sitting at the feet of Jesus.

It is interesting to note Jesus' words to Martha here: "*Are they really that important?*" The hosting tasks Martha was distracted by were not really important compared to being with Jesus at His feet. How often are we distracted by the circumstances we find ourselves facing? Sometimes the enemy uses our busyness to pull us away from Jesus' feet and a palace perspective. The point is, there is nothing more important than being at the feet of Jesus.

However, Jesus' words to Martha are words of love, acceptance and affirmation: "*Martha, my beloved Martha*". You can almost hear the gentleness in His voice. You can hear the longing in His voice for Martha to realise that at His feet distractions disappear. The distractions are nothing in comparison to what Mary chose. Jesus is not scolding Martha; He's not pointing a finger like an angry father for doing the wrong thing. Instead, Jesus is celebrating Mary's choice and He's encouraging Martha to pause and come to the same place as Mary. He is commending Mary for choosing to rest at His feet and worship Him knowing that this was the only thing needed. He is celebrating Mary's choice to not be distracted by what was going on around her and staying focused on Him in whom she will find rest.

I want to encourage you to follow Mary's example and to come to His feet to worship Him. I want to encourage you to not let the distractions the enemy can use to keep your focus away from Jesus. At the feet of Jesus distractions, life's circumstances, whether internal or external become overshadowed by who Jesus is.

Worship shifts our focus from that which overwhelms to the One who overcomes. We become more aware of Jesus and by doing so, we can remain living from the perspective of the palace. Worship enables us to rest in Him. When we worship and minister to Jesus, as we focus on Him and gaze upon His beauty, it becomes easier to remain steadfast living in the palace.

Epilogue

My hope is that as you've read this book, for faith to have been stirred up within you that if you feel like you're in a prison, to believe there *is* a way out. I also pray you've been able to use some keys to help you to live in the fullness of life that Jesus has available for us. No matter how you may feel, I encourage you - there *is* freedom and there *is* victory.

'And God raised us up with Christ and seated us **with him** *in the heavenly realms in Christ Jesus.'*

Ephesians 2:6 (emphasis added)

God is the One who raised us up and seated us with Jesus. We are sat **with** Him. Take a moment to think this through. Jesus is sat at the right hand of the Father (Mark 16:19). This is a place of victory and rest. This is the place of completion. We are sat there with Jesus. The phrase "*with Him*" doesn't imply we are sat across from Him or in another room. To be sat with Him means to be sat together. It could literally mean sat next to Him. The Amplified Version says: "*giving us joint seating with Him.*"

If Jesus is sat in a place of victory, then it stands to reason that we too are sat in victory. Whether we feel like it or not, whether our circumstances suggest it or not, we live life from this place of victory. Notice also in this verse *where* we are sat. We are sat in heavenly places. Heaven is the place of the rulership of God. Jesus is King, and as such Heaven, in effect is His palace. We are sat with Him in His palace.

Let's look at the same verse from The Passion Translation:

'He raised us up with Christ the exalted one, and we ascended with him into the glorious perfection and authority of the heavenly realm, for we are now co-seated as one with Christ!'

Ephesians 2:6 (TPT)

It's an important and powerful truth to believe that we *have* been raised with Christ! We *have* ascended with Him into the perfection and authority of the heavenly realm. We have a place with Christ, because of Him, in heavenly places - the palace. Because of the finished work of Jesus on the Cross, we've been given the authority to be there. God has granted us access to be seated, as one, with Christ.

What does Heaven look like? Let's spend a few moments reminding ourselves of some of the facets of the culture of Heaven that we can experience when we live in the palace.

Peace

Heaven is a place of peace.

In the Kingdom of Heaven there are no wars or disagreements. There is complete unity. The triune God, the Oneness of God is just that. They are one; they are in complete agreement. They have peace and live in peace with each other. At times it may look like our circumstances are getting the better of us, but the peace of Heaven transcends them.

As Paul teaches:

'And the peace of God, which transcends all understanding will guard your hearts and minds in Christ Jesus.'

Philippians: 4:7

We don't have to let challenging circumstances overwhelm us; we don't have to fear them. Where there is peace, there is no fear. Because we live from the palace perspective we live in a place of peace.

'Peace I leave with you; my peace I give you. I do not give as the world gives. Do not let your hearts be troubled and do not be afraid.'

John 14:27

Jesus has already given us His peace. Let's live in the reality of His peace.

Freedom

Secondly, Heaven is a place of freedom.

If we believe in Jesus, then we are set free. Jesus Himself says:

'So if the Son sets you free, you will be free indeed.'

John 8:36

Notice, it is the Son who has set us free. Jesus came that we might be saved, healed, and delivered. He came that we might have life in all its fullness (John 10:10). If He has set us free, we *can* live free of the bondages that the enemy may try to trap us in. By living trapped, we are not able to live that full life Jesus promises. Living in the palace means we can live in the freedom that Jesus enabled us to live.

'It is for freedom that Christ has set us free. Stand firm, then, and do not let yourselves be burdened again by a yoke of slavery.'

Galatians 5:1

The Passion Translations says:

'…we must always cherish this truth and refuse to go back into the bondage of our past.'

Galatians 5:1b (TPT)

Let's treasure this truth and begin to live in it. We will no longer go back to being captive. We are able to live free.

Victory
Thirdly, Heaven is a place of victory.

'But thanks be to God! He gives us the victory through our Lord Jesus Christ.'

1 Corinthians 15:57

Jesus has given us everything we need be victorious and conquer those things that hold us back. When Jesus declared "*It is finished*" (John 19:30), He was proclaiming that the enemy was defeated. Everything the enemy might throw at us can be overcome. This cry of Jesus is our cry too. We can say to the prison *"It is finished"*. We have the victory. In the prison we often feel we live life defeated, however, Jesus has the key to victory, and He gives it to us. As we live from the palace, we can live in the reality of victory.

Hope
Fourthly, Heaven is a place of hope.

Look at how Paul describes Jesus:

'Paul, an apostle of Christ Jesus by the command of God our saviour and of Christ ***Jesus our hope****.'*

1 Tim 1:1 (emphasis added)

Hope is not an abstract concept. Hope is a person. Jesus is our hope and He gives us hope.

Paul also encourages us in Romans:

'May the God of hope fill you with all joy and peace as you trust in him, so that you may overflow with hope by the power of the Holy Spirit'

Romans 15:13

The One who is hope, Jesus, fills us with joy and peace so that we overflow with hope. There is an abundance of hope that we can experience. The Passion Translation says:

'Now may God, the inspiration and fountain of hope, fill you to overflowing with uncontainable joy and perfect peace as you trust in him. And may the power of the Holy Spirit continually surround your life with super abundance until you radiate with hope.'

Romans 15:13 (TPT)

As we live from the palace let's radiate hope. Let our lives be full to the brim and overflowing with the hope of Heaven. Let's put our trust in the One who is trustworthy and as we do, He will inspire us to live in hope. Hope and trust go hand in hand.

Rest

Heaven is a place of rest.

There is an invitation to receive and live in His rest:

'Come to me, all you who are burdened, and I will give you rest.'

Matthew 11:28

Jesus is inviting us to come to Him. He offers us rest. To rest means to stop or to remain in a place. When we are resting, we are not toiling. When we rest we begin to recharge and be refreshed.

As we read this same verse in The Passion Translation, along with the following verse, we begin to understand how and why we are to receive this rest:

'Are you weary, carrying a heavy burden? Then come to me. I will refresh your life, for I am your oasis. Simply join your life with mine. Learn my ways and you'll discover that I'm gentle, humble and easy to please. You will find refreshment and rest in me.'

Matthew 11:28-29 (TPT)

Jesus is saying we can receive rest and refreshment from our burdens. We do this by joining our life with His. In other words, pursue intimacy with Jesus and partner with what Heaven has for us. To live in the reality of Heaven is to simply live in the palace. We are being encouraged to remain in the palace, for it is only in Jesus there is complete rest.

Heaven is the palace, and it is the place we are already seated. Let's determine to live our lives from that place – the palace!

Afterword

Throughout the course of reading this book you may have thought *'I've tried so many of these ideas, I've tried different keys, yet still I continue to battle with the same thoughts. I still feel as though I am living with a prison mindset.'*

I want to firstly honour you for where you are at. I accept that sometimes it is easier said than done. I completely understand there are times a prison can feel so tightly closed in around us that it seems there is no escape.

I recognise that the keys I have talked about in this book are only a small number of many. They are keys that I have found helpful in my personal ongoing journey to greater freedom; I recognise there may be other keys that might be helpful to you. I want to bless you to receive revelation from God about which keys to use on your ongoing journey into greater freedom in your life.

In both this book and my first, I have mentioned the Bethel Sozo ministry. I encourage people who are feeling they are in prison to book an appointment. In the UK you can find more details at www.bethelsozouk.org.uk. Some of the prayer ministry methods I have described in this book are based on this ministry.

A Sozo aims to establish a stronger, more intimate connection between you and each member of the Trinity. It is in an inner healing ministry which addresses heart wounds that may have caused us to feel like we are imprisoned and subsequent negative mindsets that may have developed. In a Sozo God may highlight lies that you have begun to believe about yourself or Him. As a guest goes through a session God reveals what His thoughts and truths are, and the door to the prison you are in not only opens up, but you can begin to walk free.

I remember a time I was leading a Sozo session where the guest felt they were caged up. After the session the guest described feeling "*lighter than air*" and that they had been uncaged.

Just as there may be different keys for you to walk into your freedom, there may be other ministries that can assist you in experiencing greater freedom. There is no 'one size fits all'. There are many other powerful inner healing and freedom ministries and counselling services available that can be helpful as you continue to pursue greater freedom.

When you experience new freedom, it is important to walk it out. Just like someone who has done their time in prison and is released, they then have to learn to walk out their new freedom. A friend of mine who used to experience anger once said that after a Sozo they realised there was now a 'firewall' between the anger and their reaction. In other words, they now had a choice to partner with anger and react accordingly, or they could choose not to. My friend continually chooses not to partner with anger. Before, they felt like there was no choice, there was no firewall. But now there is, and this enabled them to walk free. My friend is one of the calmest people I know.

As with the prisoner who is released, if my friend doesn't walk in his new freedom and returns to his previous behaviours and way of thinking, they are likely to return to that same prison.

Whatever the prison you have experienced, it is important that you now apply that freedom to your life. It might be daily declaring a truth; it might be recognising the choice you now have, or it might be something from this book.

Whatever the keys for you are, I hope this book has encouraged you to be able to begin to break free, to recognise that the prison is not your home, and there *is* hope, freedom and breakthrough. There is nothing Jesus is not able to break you free from. There is nothing that He has not defeated.

'So if the Son sets you free, you will be free indeed.'

John 8:36

Appendix

These are some of the truths about our identity found in the Bible:

I am a saint not a sinner. (Romans 1:7)

When God looks at me, He sees me as holy and blameless. (Ephesians 1:4)

I am precious and a treasured possession to God. (Deuteronomy 14:2)

I am an important member of God's royal family. (1 Peter 2:9)

I am seated in Heavenly places with Jesus right now. (Ephesians 2:6)

I am beautiful, I have been wonderfully made. (Psalms 139)

I am more than a conqueror. (Romans 8:37)

I can think like Jesus because I have the mind of Christ. (Philippians 2:5)

God's power living in me means I am not timid, but I am powerful. (2 Timothy 1:7)

I am an heir of God Himself. (Romans 8:17)

I am not a mistake, God planned for me and every day of my life. (Psalms 139:16)

I have a God-ordained purpose in life. (Jeremiah 29:11)

I am victorious. (1 Corinthians 15:57)

I have authority to overcome the enemy. (Luke 10:19)